JB JOSSEY-BASS

Grant Proposal Makeover

TRANSFORM YOUR REQUEST

FROM NO TO YES

Here's to YES!

Cheryl A. Clarke
Susan P. Fox

BICENTENNIAL
1807
WILEY
2007
BICENTENNIAL

John Wiley & Sons, Inc.

Published by Jossey-Bass
A Wiley Imprint
989 Market Street, San Francisco, CA 94103-1741   www.josseybass.com

Jossey-Bass books and products are available through most bookstores. To contact Jossey-Bass directly call our Customer Care Department within the U.S. at 800-956-7739, outside the U.S. at 317-572-3986 or fax 317-572-4002.

Jossey-Bass also publishes its books in a variety of electronic formats. Some content that appears in print may not be available in electronic books.

Library of Congress Cataloging-in-Publication Data

Clarke, Cheryl, date.
Grant proposal makeover : transform your request from no to yes / Cheryl A. Clarke, Susan P. Fox. —
1st ed.
  p. cm.
Includes index.
ISBN-13: 978-0-7879-8055-9 (pbk.)
ISBN-10: 0-7879-8055-2 (pbk.)
1. Proposal writing for grants. I. Fox, Susan P., date. II. Title.
HV41.2C518 2007
658.15'224—dc22   2006030496

Printed in the United States of America
FIRST EDITION
PB Printing 10 9 8 7 6 5 4 3 2 1

CONTENTS

Preface v

The Authors ix

Introduction 1

1 Demonstrating the Fit: Making First and Lasting Impressions 5

2 Disorganized Proposals: Bringing Order to the Chaos 21

3 The Case of the Missing Needs Statement:
Honing the Heart of the Proposal 51

4 Too Much of a Good Thing: Taming the Statistician 69

5 Evaluation: Making Sure the Proposal Measures Up 83

6 Budgets: Telling Your Story in Dollars and Cents 101

7 Proposal Length: The Long and Short of It 113

8 Split Personality: What Happens When There's More
Than One Writer 127

9 Florid Writing: When Proposals Go Over the Top 151

10 The "Mystery" Proposal: Making Sense of Nonsense 167

11 The Perfect Package 185

Mission Accomplished: Transformation Complete 195

Resource A: Checklist for a Memorandum of Understanding 199

Resource B: Grantmakers Responding to Our Survey 203

Index 207

This book is dedicated to Susan's baby granddaughter,

Catherine Santos Fox, born during the gestation of this book,

and to Cheryl's daughter, Hannah Clarke Schwalbe,

who entered her teen years during the same period.

Both are perfect in every way and will never need a makeover.

PREFACE

A makeover craze is sweeping across America. From faces to houses, transformations are taking place, often in front of a TV audience. Although we cannot deny that contemporary culture influenced our book's title, *Grant Proposal Makeover* is actually more seriously rooted. Over the years, we've read a great many books on proposal writing that *tell* the reader what to do and what not to do when drafting a proposal. But resources are scarce when it comes to *showing* the reader what to do and how to do it, especially when it comes to editing proposals. Our book does just that. What we've done, with input from respected program officers from across the country, is identify the most common problems found in grant proposals. The problems identified ranged from those of style to those of substance. They include disorganized proposals; florid writing; abstract, vague, pontificating writing; narratives that are too long; narratives that are too short; proposals that do not fully or adequately describe the problem or need; those packed with irrelevant statistics; and those where the accompanying budget raises more questions than it provides answers. In each chapter, we give you a sample proposal—an "ugly duckling"—that demonstrates one of these specific problems. We point out the flaws, and we explain why funders view the defect as a handicap in awarding funds. We include quotes from the program officers themselves, which shed more light on what they specifically like and don't like in proposal narratives. Then we transform the "ugly duckling" proposal into a "beautiful swan," so you can see how to correct these common mistakes.

By seeing it all—the good, the bad, and the ugly—you should have an easier time editing your own proposals, as well as those written by others, making your submissions easier for grantmakers to understand—and to fund. In other words, we show you how to transform your requests from *no* to *yes*. That's why you're reading this book in the first place—to increase the likelihood that your proposals will be awarded funding for your agency and its worthwhile programs.

We are aware of the many fine resources—books and workshops—that provide valuable assistance in helping writers construct a proposal from the ground up. Our book differs in that we show you how to successfully "remodel" a flawed proposal. After assessing what's currently in the marketplace, we believe this is a novel approach and one that will benefit the beginning grantwriter as well as the seasoned professional.

THE PROPOSAL: A MEANS TO AN END

We are also aware of and want to emphasize the proper role the proposal plays in the overall grantseeking process. A written request for funding—a proposal—is one key step in the process, but not the *only* step. We do not want to overstate the importance of a proposal, nor do we wish to minimize it.

Some have made the analogy that a grant proposal is similar to a resume. We believe this is a valid comparison. A resume is something every job seeker must have. Much time and energy are appropriately devoted to crafting an effective résumé, one that showcases the job seeker's strengths (namely, skills, knowledge, expertise, and experience) and communicates to the employer that the job seeker is an excellent candidate for the position. Similarly, a proposal presents an agency's strengths by describing its past achievements, discussing its current programs, and demonstrating that it has a plan for future sustainability. Much like a resume, a proposal communicates to the potential funder that the applicant is an excellent candidate, though with a proposal this is for funding rather than a job.

Let's take this analogy a step further. A resume by itself, no matter how strong, is unlikely to secure a job for the applicant. Strategic job seekers will first research potential employers to determine which companies will enable them to best utilize their skills and expertise. Strategic grantseekers do the same thing: they research and identify those funders who are most likely to financially support their agencies. Both types of applicants (that is, those seeking jobs and those seeking funds) may have opportunities to make personal connections with individuals associated with the potential employer or funder. Eventually, a resume or proposal is likely to be submitted.

The proposal, like a resume, is a single step in a larger, more complex process. However, because crafting a strong proposal is such an important step, books have been written and workshops have been presented about how to do the step well. We believe our book adds helpful new information to the field of grantseeking and will be useful to those of you who write proposals and those of you who review them.

WHAT'S AHEAD?

In our first chapter, we use the "short story" of proposal writing—the letter of inquiry—to demonstrate how to establish your agency's "fit" with the prospective funder. Convincing grantmakers that your project fits within their guidelines and funding priorities will have a big impact on your success in winning grants.

In Chapter Two, we transform a disorganized proposal into one that follows a logical order and sequence. The following four chapters mirror that sequence and are ordered in the typical structure of grant proposal. Chapter Three identifies the missing need, and Chapter Four discusses the appropriate use of statistics and data in the Needs Statement. In Chapters Five and Six, we examine the crucial role of evaluations and budgets that accompany proposal narratives.

Our concluding chapters focus on different stylistic challenges that pose problems for grantseekers, such as writing too much or too little, florid prose, writing "by committee," and narratives that are too abstract or academic. We conclude with a chapter on the proper packaging of a proposal and a summary.

As you read this book, pay particular attention to those chapters that describe flaws you may be susceptible to in writing proposals. Our intention is to give you the tools needed to avoid writing "ugly ducklings" when you intended to draft "beautiful swans" and to have the skills to successfully remodel a "fixer-upper" when necessary.

September 2006

Cheryl A. Clarke
Mill Valley, California

Susan P. Fox
San Francisco, California

THE AUTHORS

Cheryl A. Clarke is a fundraising consultant, trainer, and author. She is the author of *Storytelling for Grantseekers: The Guide to Creative Nonprofit Fundraising,* Jossey-Bass, 2001. A self-described "recovering lawyer," Clarke works with nonprofit organizations throughout Northern California to improve their fundraising capacity. Recent clients include: Shanti, St. Mary's Medical Center, the San Francisco International Music Festival, Jesuit Volunteer Corps: Southwest, and the Redwoods Retirement Center.

Clarke also regularly teaches workshops in basic fundraising techniques and grantwriting both locally and nationally. She is a featured trainer at CompassPoint Nonprofit Services. Together with coauthor Susan P. Fox, she has co-moderated the highly regarded Reality Grantmaking workshops at local Association of Fundraising Professionals (AFP) conferences, Craigslist Nonprofit Bootcamp, CompassPoint Nonprofit Services Peninsula and East Bay Funders Fairs, and the Center for Volunteer & Nonprofit Leadership. Clarke and Fox were co-presenters at the 2006 AFP International Conference.

Clarke is a member of the Association of Fundraising Professionals and served as the Golden Gate Chapter's vice president for education for two years and as a board member for three years. She currently serves on the board of directors of the Development Executives Roundtable and is a member of the American Association of Grant Professionals. Over the years, she has also been active in the community, serving on many boards of directors and volunteering at her daughter's school. In her free time, she writes short fiction and has been published in several literary magazines, including *Potpourri* and *Bust Out Stories.*

Prior to establishing her consulting practice in 1995, Clarke held development positions at The Marine Mammal Center, University of California-San Francisco, and the University of San Francisco School of Law. She has a bachelor of science in journalism from Northwestern University and a law degree from the University of San Francisco School of Law.

Susan P. Fox has worked as an independent fundraising consultant to nonprofit organizations since 1980 and has held the designation of certified fundraising executive (CFRE) since 1995. She has served as development director at Salem Lutheran Home in Oakland, California, and at The Management Center in San Francisco.

As a consultant, she provides services in strategic fundraising, including grantwriting, appeal letter writing, public relations, major donor campaigns, feasibility studies, and development audits, as well as training in major gifts, grantsmanship, annual fund, and planned giving campaigns. Recent clients include the Alameda County Health Care Foundation, the Taproot Foundation, the Lions Center for the Visually Impaired of Diablo Valley, and School-to-School International.

Based in San Francisco, Fox frequently leads workshops on fundraising throughout the United States and Mexico and has been an instructor at University of California-Berkeley Extension, University of San Francisco, and University of Montana. With her colleague Cheryl A. Clarke, she organizes and co-moderates popular Reality Grantmaking workshops at several San Francisco Bay Area conferences. She is also a regular trainer at CompassPoint Nonprofit Services.

Fox is a member of the Association of Fundraising Professionals and served on the board of its Golden Gate Chapter for two years, including one year as vice president for education. She currently serves on the board of directors of Development Executives Roundtable and is a member of the American Association of Grant Professionals. In her free time, she enjoys reading, gardening, hiking, and spending time with her family.

A fourth-generation native San Franciscan, she holds a bachelor of arts degree in psychology from the University of San Francisco.

Future collaborations by Clarke and Fox include joint consulting engagements, workshops and trainings, and writing projects.

INTRODUCTION

When we began working on this book, we already had a pretty good idea of what issues we would focus on to show the transformation of "ugly duckling" proposals into "beautiful swans." Between us, we have more than forty years of experience in writing and rewriting grant proposals. We've also done quite a bit of teaching on the topic of grantwriting. Over the years, we've seen quite a few proposals that just didn't do an adequate, much less spectacular, job.

But our opinion on what makes the difference between proposals that win grants and those that don't are just that: our opinions. The people whose opinions really count are the grantmakers who read proposals, make funding recommendations, and award grants.

ADVICE FROM THE "OTHER SIDE OF THE DESK"

Over the past several years, we've had a unique opportunity to hear firsthand the comments of grantmakers reviewing proposals through a series of Reality Grantmaking workshops that we organized at various conferences throughout Northern California.

As we prepared to write this book, our editors suggested that we might want to gather more feedback from funders so that we could quote them in our book and validate the advice we were planning to give. We recognized that this was also a way to do a reality check on our own notions about what helps a proposal effectively communicate the case for support to grantmakers and what makes proposals difficult to read and understand.

Our purpose in polling grantmakers was to verify that our ideas for the book's content were valid and to gather some informal feedback on the issues we planned to address. Neither of us has a background in survey methodology, and we weren't envisioning more than a dozen or so e-mails or phone calls to people we knew in the funding world to gather some anecdotal evidence and ideally some good quotes to use in our book.

We started by drawing up a list of questions to ask funders. Some required simple yes-or-no answers and some were multiple choice. We also included a few open-ended questions in order to generate valuable quotes for inclusion in our narrative. We asked funders what bugs them the most in proposals coming in over the transom. We solicited their feedback about different writing styles. We questioned them about specific parts of the typical proposal. We inquired about their preferences for formatting, presentation, attachments, and budgets. We even asked them how they thought proposals should be delivered.

We tried out the survey by e-mailing the questions to a few of our colleagues who are grantmakers. We asked them for feedback on the questionnaire. How long did it take them to complete it? Did they have suggestions for improvements? Who else should we send it to? And most important, were we asking the right questions? We know that grantmakers are busy people, and we wanted to make it as painless as possible for them to give us what we were looking for.

We are very grateful to those "early responders" for the valuable advice they gave and for the dozens of colleagues they suggested we send the survey to. Somewhere in this process, a couple of people mentioned Grantmakers for Effective Organizations and suggested we contact them. When we did, they were gracious enough to circulate the survey via one of their e-mail listserves. The response from grantmakers throughout the country, and even a few from Canada, dramatically improved the geographical scope of the responses.

The size of our survey pool grew to sixty-nine funders and the geographical spread expanded significantly, but the survey results cannot be considered scientific evidence. The opinions we gathered remain anecdotal indications of grantmaker preferences.

MEET THE GRANTMAKERS

Who were the people who responded to our survey? They represent a cross section of the funding world. As we expected, most of them (twenty-five out of sixty-nine) are based in California, where we work. Of the rest, 20 percent are from the Northeast, 40 percent from the Midwest, 20 percent from the South, and 20 percent from other states in the West.

Respondents represent community foundations, private family foundations, and public charities. Some limit their grantmaking to one field of service, like health or the arts or children. Others make grants across several categories. One only makes grants to individuals, and one awards services and not cash. Respondents reported from one to thirty years of experience in reviewing proposals. More than three-quarters of them have worked for grantseeking nonprofits, and 91 percent have written proposals as grant applicants themselves. Some are executive directors or CEOs. Others are program officers or grants managers. At least one is a foundation trustee.

We are delighted that sixty-nine funders took the time to respond. And we were especially pleased that so many of them commented, sometimes at length, in response to issues we raised. We hope the grantmaker comments we share in the pages ahead are instructive for you.

We give a complete list of those who responded to the survey at the back of the book, in Resource B.

ABOUT THE PROPOSALS

In planning this book, we quickly realized that no grantwriter would willingly put forth for public review their poorly written or disorganized proposals. Given this reality and facing the task of isolating specific proposal problems and then effectively correcting them, we decided we needed to write all the proposal examples— the "ugly ducklings" as well as the "beautiful swans"—presented in this book. They are based on flawed proposals we have encountered in our work, but the organizations, the staffs, and the programs described are all inventions of our imagination. We chose, however, to review these proposals in the third person. This approach enabled us to critique our own work with a more critical eye—with an eye for providing you with the most helpful tools for constructing your own perfect proposals.

Demonstrating the Fit
Making First and Lasting Impressions

S top! Take your fingers off the keyboard and step away from the computer monitor.

Before you write that first word in a letter of inquiry or grant proposal, you must assess whether or not your agency (and the program or project you're seeking funding for) is a good fit with the grantmaker. If you've determined that the fit is solid, then you may return to the computer and begin writing. However, if you're unsure or have doubts, you either don't have a strong match or you'll need to investigate further to determine if you do.

FITNESS IS FOUND IN THE GUIDELINES

Grantmakers want to make it as easy as possible for potential applicants to figure out whether or not they should apply for funding. This is because funders do not want to receive a lot of proposals that are not aligned with their funding priorities and therefore fall outside their guidelines. That's why the majority of grantmakers publish guidelines on their Web sites or in a hard copy format that can be snail-mailed to potential applicants.

It is essential that you obtain a copy of a funder's *most current* guidelines and thoroughly review them before beginning to prepare a grant application. Guidelines will help you determine whether or not your agency (and the program or project for which funding is sought) fits like Cinderella's slipper with a given funder. This is because most guidelines are pretty clear about specifying what the grantmaker will or will not fund.

Before a foundation, corporation, or other grantmaking entity awards its very first grant, the decision makers at the funding agency will have thoughtfully considered, internally debated, and ultimately concluded what types of nonprofit agencies, programs, and projects will be eligible for funding. Decisions can be driven by the interests of the founders or by an awareness of urgent community needs. Even with the very largest grantmakers, it is impractical to open the doors to every type of nonprofit agency anywhere in the world. Instead funders focus. They focus on addressing specific problems or unmet community needs. They set geographical limitations. They limit funding to certain types of financial requests (for example, general operating support, program or project, capital and equipment, endowments, scholarships, and the like). These preferences are almost always specified in a funder's guidelines. "*Fit*" is an alignment with these preferences.

In addition to reading the guidelines, you should also review a list of a funder's current and recent grantees. These grantee agencies already have successfully proven their "fit" with the funding agency. Who and what has been funded in the recent past is an excellent indicator of who and what the grantmaker is likely to support in the near future. Please keep in mind that grantmakers can and do change their funding priorities, which is why we obtain *current* guidelines and review *recent* grantees.

"The proposal writer should take time to investigate the guidelines and look at past grantees to assess the likelihood of consideration," says Lori McGlinchey of the Open Society Institute.

THE FOUR FITNESS FACTORS

Several factors determine fit. The most important are subject matter, geography, type of financial need, and grant amount. When evaluating a foundation, corporation, government agency, or other grantmaker as a potential grantor for your agency, consider the following questions:

1. Is your agency's mission and purpose a funding priority of the grantmaker?
2. Does the grantmaker fund in the geographical area where your agency is located or where it serves its clients?
3. Does the grantmaker make grants for what your agency seeks funding for— for example, general operating support, program or project support, scholarships, endowment, capital improvements, and so forth?

4. Does the dollar amount your agency seeks fall within the range of grants typically awarded by the grantmaker?

If—and only if—you answered yes to each of these questions, then there is an apparent alignment between your agency and the grantmaker. Now you may proceed to approach the funder for support by writing that letter of inquiry or a full proposal. The format of the initial approach, whether a letter of inquiry or formal proposal, depends on the preference of the grantmaker.

Some grantmakers require that a letter of inquiry precede the submission of a formal proposal. Generally, these letters are one to three pages in length and are used by the funder as a screening device. Successful letters of inquiry will be rewarded with an invitation to the nonprofit organization to submit a full proposal. Recipients of unsuccessful letters of inquiry need not apply.

In your initial written submission to a funder, be it in a letter of inquiry or a full proposal, it is essential to demonstrate fit and to make a positive first impression. Then the question becomes this: To what extent should applicants go to demonstrate that their nonprofit organization and program or project is a good fit with a potential funder?

PARROT BACK?

Conventional wisdom may tell us to mirror the language in the funder's guidelines. Parrot back the grantmaker's own words is the advice offered by many trainers of grantwriting workshops and in dozens of books on "how to write successful grant proposals."

This is precisely the advice followed in the following example. Read the guidelines for the fictitious Anderson Family Foundation and then the responding letter of inquiry from the fictitious nonprofit organization, Bridges to Nature. As you read, consider whether the writer has adequately demonstrated the fit and made a positive first impression.

SAMPLE FOUNDATION GUIDELINES

In the pages ahead, the potential grantee is responding to the following guidelines from the fictitious Anderson Family Foundation.

ANDERSON FAMILY FOUNDATION: GUIDELINES FOR APPLICANTS

Who We Are

The Anderson Family Foundation is a small but growing family foundation that strives to make a difference in the local community, which has been home to four generations of Andersons. Our values are expressed in our grantmaking, which emphasizes enlightenment of the mind, empowerment of the individual, nurturing of creativity and expression, and respect for and appreciation of nature and wildlife. To this end, we are dedicated to the well-being of children and youth, with special interest in programs that cultivate a better understanding of the natural world and foster creativity. The Foundation takes an avid interest in safeguarding our environment for future generations. Environmental education is critical if society is to preserve and protect natural resources. We believe that each individual can make a difference, and although society's problems can appear overwhelming, we see great hope in the enthusiasm, creativity, and intelligence of young people. The Foundation seeks opportunities where small and medium-sized grants can have a deep and lasting impact.

What We Fund

- Nonprofit agencies and their programs that (1) benefit children and youth, particularly young people from low-income households and those at risk within the Greater Urban City four-county area (Forest, Hill, Marsh, and River Counties) and (2) provide environmental education to children and youth

- General operating, program, and project support

- Grants in the range of $10,000 to $50,000

- Agencies that do not discriminate against any person or group on the basis of age, race, gender, ethnicity, disability, religion, national origin, political affiliation, or sexual orientation

- 501(c)(3) organizations or those with a fiscal sponsor

What We Do Not Fund

- Capital campaigns, endowments, scholarships, individuals, films, videos, conferences, or fundraising events
- Multiyear funding requests

What Is Our Process

The Foundation accepts two-page letters of inquiry throughout the year. Those selected will be invited to submit a formal application.

Send letters to:
    Judi Smyth
    Grants Manager
    Anderson Family Foundation
    100 Main Street
    Suburbia, CA 90000-0001

January 30, 2006
Ms. Judy Smith
Grants Manager
Anderson Family Foundation
100 Main Street
Suburbia, CA 90000-0001

Dear Ms. Smith:

I am writing this letter of inquiry to the Anderson Family Foundation to tell you about Bridges to Nature, a unique and innovative 501(c)(3) not-for-profit organization that serves the Greater Urban City four-county area. Bridges to Nature is a wildlife sanctuary with year-round programming that educates children and youth about our natural world and fosters their creativity. We believe that Bridges to Nature is a good fit with the Anderson Family Foundation because our programs enlighten the mind, empower the individual, nurture creativity and expression, and teach respect for nature and wildlife. If invited to submit a full proposal, we would request grant funding of between $10,000 and $50,000. These funds will have a deep and lasting impact on the at-risk and disenfranchised youth we serve.

At Bridges to Nature, we seek to safeguard nature and wildlife from suburban development, and inspire future generations to preserve and protect our natural resources. Founded in 1985, Bridges to Nature is celebrating our 20th anniversary of providing young people with a better understanding of the natural world. We believe that each individual child can make a difference. While problems such as suburban encroachment and rampart development, and the accompanying loss of wildlife habitat and wildlife itself, can appear overwhelming, we see great hope in the enthusiasm, creativity and intelligence of young people.

Bridges to Nature needs grant support to underwrite the costs of our educational programs for low-income and at-risk youth. Since our founding, we have opened our sanctuary gates to hundreds of school groups. Schoolchildren visit our beautiful 350-acre site located in forested hills that are populated by dozens of varieties of birds, deer, raccoons, skunks, bobcats, and the occasional mountain lion. Though Bridges to Nature is only a 30-minute drive from Urban City, the majority of low-income and at-risk youth have never experienced it. We introduce these young people to a whole new world that is beyond their daily experience. Our short-term goal is to provide children with an understanding of, and appreciation for, nature that they will cherish all their lives. Our long-term goal is to develop citizens who will help safeguard our environment for future generations.

Severe cuts have had a negative affect on school district budgets, causing many schools to eliminate field trips because bus transportation and related expenses cost too much. Bridges to Nature seeks grant funding so school children in poor and under-funded school districts continue to have opportunities to visit nature. We have to raise at least $10,000 in support to sustain this program in the coming year, as current grant funding is about to run out.

We hope that the Anderson Family Foundation will want to learn more about Bridges to Nature. Please advice us as to whether we should submit a formal grant proposal. Thank you very much for your consideration.

Sincerely,

Chiaki Yamamoto-Barron

Chiaki Yamamoto-Barron, Executive Director

Problem Number One: No Fit-Ness

There are several problems with this sample letter. Let's begin with how the letter attempts to demonstrate fit. See how the applicant repeats the funder's exact words and phrases almost to the letter.

- "enlighten the mind, empower the individual, nurture creativity and expression, and teach respect for nature and wildlife"
- "We believe that each individual [child] can make a difference"
- "While problems . . . can appear overwhelming"
- "[These funds will have] a deep and lasting impact."

It's almost as if the foundation officer rather than the grant applicant wrote the letter, for it tells us more about the foundation than it does about Bridges to Nature. This letter doesn't give us any feel for the agency's personality and passion. It doesn't talk about the people involved or what the youth participants in Bridges to Nature do when they visit the sanctuary. Certainly, the letter doesn't capture the essence of Bridges to Nature and captivate the reader. This is one of the dangers in simply parroting back the funder's own words.

What this letter offers is an excellent example of *TELLING* about fit without really *SHOWING* it. That's a serious omission. The best stories (and we believe that letters of inquiry and grant proposals should tell good stories) are those that *show*, not *tell*.

Are we flying in the face of conventional wisdom? According to each of the survey respondents who commented on this topic, the conventional wisdom is wrong. Here's what a few of the funders had to say:

"I know every grantwriter is told to mirror the language in an RFP [Request for Proposal]. I have found that more often than not, the more mirroring of language there is, the less actual fit there is." (Aaron Jacobs, Program Officer, Social Venture Partners, Seattle)

"Mirroring the language in the guidelines tells me that they are trying to fit, but makes me wonder if they have really thought about that fit." (Mary Gregory, program officer at Pacific Foundation Services, a small San Francisco firm that manages eight family foundations)

"They should write as if they have read our guidelines, but without parroting what we have said." (Sandra Sinclair, The J. W. McConnell Family Foundation)

Further, Ricardo Millett of the Woods Fund of Chicago notes that his pet peeve is those "grantseekers who mimic foundation language and fail to advance their ask in their own authentic language and experience."

> **GRANTWRITING TIP!**
> *Telling* a grantmaker your agency is a good fit is *never* as strong or convincing as *showing* that your agency is a fit.

Problem Number Two: First and Lasting Mis-Impression

There are other problems with the ugly duckling letter of inquiry from Bridges to Nature to the Anderson Family Foundation. The most notable of these is the poor first impression it makes, for two reasons. First, the writer failed to spell the grants manager's name correctly. As clearly stated in the guidelines, her name is *Judi Smyth,* not *Judy Smith.* Second, there are several glaring errors in the body of the letter. No doubt the writer meant *rampant* not *rampart, advise* not *advice,* and *effect* not *affect.* But these mistakes could have been avoided if the writer had paid more attention to the details. And the devil's always in the details!

Attention to detail is critical in proposal writing. Use the spell check function on your computer. Proof your own copy, and then have another pair or two of eyes proof it as well. And *always* double-check the spelling of the program officer's name—and the name of the foundation too!

We asked the funders we surveyed what their pet peeves in grant proposals were. Several mentioned misspellings, poor grammar, and cover letters that begin with "Dear Sir or Madam" rather than with the program officer's name.

"When proposals haven't been proofed and another foundation's name is in the proposal." (Nancy Wiltsek, Pottruck Family Foundation)

"Requests that do not include contact information—address and telephone numbers—or are addressed to another program officer reflect that they have not read our guidelines." (Mario P. Diaz, Wells Fargo Foundation)

Although none of our respondents indicated that these errors standing alone were fatal flaws—misspellings, poor grammar, and getting the program officer's name wrong—they do not make a very positive first impression, and they may leave a lingering poor one. They may raise doubt in the funder's mind about whether or not the applicant agency also will be careless in delivering client services or in managing grant funding wisely. Given the competitive grants environment, why plant seeds of doubt?

> **GRANTWRITING TIP!**
> Spend a few extra minutes checking and proofing your work!

Problem Number Three: Where's the Zing?

The third major problem with the "before" letter concerns writing style and word choice. The writing is generally flat and uninspired. The letter lacks a strong opening sentence to engage the reader and segue into a compelling, persuasive story. "I am writing this letter . . ." is at best serviceable, but certainly not engaging. Sentences lack energy. Overall, the language is rather ho-hum and not likely to grab the attention of a program officer who is reading through a stack of a hundred or more letters of inquiry. Your letter has got to stand out!

Problem Number Four: Where's the Beef? and How Much Is It?

In addition to lacking zing, the letter also lacks relevant, substantive details. The reader is not told how many school children have been served by Bridges to Nature in prior years nor how many will be served in future months. No name is provided for the program for which funding is sought. There are no specifics regarding the transportation costs. No information is given about how the program was started and its financial history.

The letter fails to specify an exact grant amount, should the agency be invited to submit a full proposal. Rather, it simply repeats the Anderson Family Foundation's stated grant range of $10,000 to $50,000. In the second to the last paragraph, it is curious that the letter mentions that grant funding is about to run out but fails to mention who previously has been funding the program.

One of the cardinal rules of successful grantwriting is to leave no obvious question unanswered. Aren't you left at the end of this letter with unanswered questions?

TIME FOR A MAKEOVER

Fortunately, these problems are not hard to fix. Take a look at the following "beautiful swan" version of the Bridges to Nature letter to the Anderson Family Foundation.

January 30, 2006
Ms. Judi Smyth
Grants Manager
Anderson Family Foundation
100 Main Street
Suburbia, CA 90000-0001

Dear Ms. Smyth:

Many low-income and at-risk children living in Urban City have never seen a deer in the wild or fresh bobcat tracks in the soft dirt. At Bridges to Nature, a wildlife sanctuary and education center located a mere 30 minutes from Urban City, we give these young people an opportunity to experience nature—up close and personal!

I am writing to the Anderson Family Foundation to tell you about Bridges to Nature and our outstanding education programs. After reviewing your current guidelines, I believe that our agency is a good fit with the Foundation's funding priorities. If invited to submit a full proposal, we will ask the Foundation for a grant of $15,000 to help support our Busloads to Bridges program. This program enables underfunded schools and school districts in the Greater Urban City four-county area, though primarily in Urban City, to send school groups to Bridges to Nature.

Bridges to Nature is a 501(c)(3) not-for-profit organization founded in 1985, when the Fisher family donated 350 acres to the new agency with the stipulation that the land be held in perpetuity as a wildlife sanctuary and environmental educational center. Our educational center and small wildlife museum are housed in what was formerly the Fisher estate home. Agency offices are found in several small outbuildings near the main center.

For 20 years, Bridges to Nature has offered a variety of environmental education programs geared to elementary and high school students. We estimate that Bridges to Nature has served more than 60,000 students in the past 20 years, or an average of about 3,000 students per year. Approximately 40% of the visiting students come from low-income households. The majority of our programs are daylong visits to our sanctuary, which combine hands-on nature experiences with classroom learning. We also provide teachers with pre- and post-visit curriculum materials, which enhance the student's visit. In addition to our one-day program, Bridges to Nature also offers several multiday and weeklong options.

Several schools have brought their students each year since our educational programs were first offered. However, in recent years, we started hearing from principals and teachers that schools could no longer afford to participate due to severe budget cuts that eliminated costs such as bus rentals and even modest participation fees. Hardest hit were schools in low-income communities, especially those in Urban City, where children were the least likely to have opportunities for excursions outside the city or even outside their immediate neighborhoods. Without Bridges to Nature, these students would miss the chance to experience and learn about the natural world that exists just outside the city limits.

To meet this need, Busloads to Bridges was created three years ago with a three-year $100,000 seed grant from the Urban City Community Foundation. This funding enabled Bridges to Nature to underwrite the cost of bus transportation and group participation fees for those schools otherwise unable to bring student groups out to the sanctuary. The program has been a huge success, as all underwritten spots filled within a few weeks after notices were mailed to local schools. However, Bridges to Nature is now in the third year of the three-year grant from the Community Foundation, and we must secure new grant funding if we are to continue this worthwhile program, which is why I am writing to the Anderson Family Foundation. A grant of $15,000 would enable us to underwrite school visits for ten classrooms. The average daily bus rental rate is $500, and our full-day student group rate is $500. Student groups average between 20 and 30 children.

For a child who has never before seen a wild male turkey in full plumage, a visit to Bridges to Nature can be an eye-opening experience. I hope you will want to learn more about Bridges to Nature and will invite us to submit a full proposal. If you have any questions or need additional information, please feel free to call me. Thank you very much for considering our letter of inquiry.

Sincerely,

Chiaki Yamamoto-Barron

Chiaki Yamamoto-Barron
Executive Director

LETTER OF INQUIRY MAKEOVER:
A PRETTIER PICTURE

This "after" version is much improved. The first sentence grabs the reader's attention with vivid mental pictures of "a deer in the wild" and "fresh bobcat tracks in the soft dirt." The program's name is provided. As a program name, *Busloads to Bridges* is both descriptive and clever. What an agency *calls* a program is important for many reasons. A name conveys information about the specific nature and activity of the program, and it also becomes verbal "shorthand" both inside and outside the agency. Therefore, careful consideration should be given to the selection of a program name.

In the revised letter, the specific amount of grant funding sought, in this case $15,000, is given. This demonstrates that the agency carefully reviewed the foundation's guidelines, saw the typical grant range, and wisely selected to request an amount within that range. As a strategic decision, the fact that the ask amount is in the lower half of the range is probably a wise one for a first-time applicant, as funders frequently award larger grants to renewing grantees. The ending completes the circle, returning the reader to a sharp visual image of "a wild male turkey in full plumage."

The makeover version of the letter also provides a bit of the agency's history, as well as information about how the program began and where funding has come from. The program itself is described with just enough relevant details for a letter of inquiry. Hard numbers show results. For example, the fact that 60,000 students have participated in the Bridges to Nature program over its 20-year history is important and relevant. A strong letter of inquiry will discuss the problem to be addressed (in this case, low-income school children who have little opportunity to experience nature and who attend school in a district that cannot afford transportation costs to take students on field trips) and the agency's proposed response (providing low-income school children with grant-funded transportation to the nature sanctuary). This letter has met both of these criteria.

Throughout the letter, the writing style and tone are also much improved. There is a faster-paced energy that was lacking in the before version. The writer has made better word choices. Each sentence pulls the reader forward to the next sentence. Yet because this is a brief letter of inquiry, there are no wasted words or sentences. But there is passion. The reader gets a feeling for the agency and a clearer idea of what the participating students do when they visit the sanctuary.

Unlike the earlier, weaker version, the revised letter answers all of the reader's obvious questions. The goal is to pique the funder's interest by providing just enough of the most relevant information, making it more likely that the funder will want to learn more and will invite the submission of a formal proposal.

Finally, the makeover version achieves the primary objective of every letter of inquiry: it demonstrates that the agency and the program fit within the grant-maker's funding priorities. And it achieves this by *showing rather than telling.*

WRAPPING UP THE FIT

Our objective for this chapter has been to help you understand the importance of demonstrating your agency's "fit" to a funder and how to do it well. Saying you fit is not enough. You must convince the grantmaker that there is an alignment of interests, and you do this by describing your agency, its mission, the unmet need and clients to be served, and how the program will fulfill this need. Let the funders be your guide:

"It really comes down to communicating strong ideas and vision clearly and succinctly." (Liesel Fenner, New England Foundation for the Arts)

"Often, connecting the proposal to the Fund's guidelines is my job," Frances Phillips, of the Walter and Elise Haas Fund, says. "I have to interpret and translate the organization's work within the foundation's priorities. It helps if the organization points to where they see the fit, but I don't want to sacrifice my opportunity to understand their mission and how diligently and thoughtfully they are addressing it."

Disorganized Proposals
Bringing Order to the Chaos

Putting a proposal together can be a lot like building or remodeling a house. There can be so many decisions, components, and steps that it's often difficult to know where and how to begin.

Often the grantmaker's guidelines will provide clear directions for how to organize your proposal. Funders will give you either (1) a list of the sections they want your proposal to include or (2) a list of questions they want your proposal to answer. Either way, you must follow the order *exactly* as it is given. Funders are sticklers about this issue. They expect to see their instructions followed to the letter. This makes it easier for reviewers to find specific information when evaluating and discussing proposals.

STANDARD SEQUENCE

Grantmakers generally want the same information and usually in about the same order. The following narrative structure is typical:

- Summary
- History and Mission of the Applicant Agency
- Description of the Problem or Need
- Agency's Goals and Objectives
- Agency's Proposed Methods
- Agency's Plan for Assessment or Evaluation
- Agency's Plan for Obtaining Future Funding and Sustainability

There's a reason why proposal narratives are generally constructed in this order. It provides a logical sequence for presenting your case for support and answering a grantmaker's usual questions.

Proposals begin with a Summary that gives a brief overview of the problem, the agency's response, and projected results. A Summary is often as short as a single paragraph and usually should be no longer than a half page. In those circumstances where the grantmaker uses an application form, a Summary may be required to fit into a certain space or be limited to as few as one or two hundred words.

Following the Summary, the proposal usually describes the agency, its mission, and its prior achievements. This section lays down a foundation of credibility for the agency, for if the nonprofit has had past successes, it is likely to succeed in the future.

Next, in the Problem or Needs Statement, the proposal discusses the clients served by the agency. These clients may be negatively affected by a societal condition or situation that the agency will address, and the agency's programs may offer their clients a unique window of opportunity. If we stay with our construction metaphor, the Needs Statement forms the walls of the proposal.

The roof goes on in the next two sections with a discussion about the agency's intended results (objectives, outcomes) and the agency's methodology. These key sections answer these twin questions: What are you going to achieve, and how are you going to do it? The finishing touches come last, with sections on evaluation and future funding. A section devoted to plans for assessment addresses the following question: How will you measure success? The last substantive section is forward looking. It provides assurances of future sustainability due to a solid fundraising plan.

To this general structure, we usually add a closing section to formally request the funding. We typically make this the final paragraph in the proposal. The purpose of this paragraph is twofold. First, it reminds the program officer how much money your agency is asking for. (Yes, this is a bit redundant, as you will have already stated your grant request in the proposal's accompanying cover letter and possibly in the Summary as well, but we find it is useful to do again.) Second, it's a tidy way to close the proposal.

In addition to the narrative, funders will also want to see a program or project budget (covered in Chapter Six), an overall agency budget, a list of the agency's board of directors, a copy of the agency's 501(c)(3) letter, audited financial statements, and various other attachments that we will cover more fully in Chapter Eleven.

IN THE FORM OF A QUESTION, PLEASE!

The previous list of proposal components, with the exception of the Proposal Summary, can be rephrased in the form of questions, as follows:

- What is the History and Mission of the agency?
- What is the Problem or Need the agency is trying to address?
- What are the agency's Goals and Objectives for meeting the Problem or Need?
- What Methods will the agency use to achieve its Goals and Objectives?
- How will the agency assess whether it achieved its Objectives? What is the agency's plan for evaluating the program's success?
- How will the agency sustain the program in the future?
- What is the agency's strategy for obtaining future funding?

The same information is being sought, whether in the form of questions or as a list of topics. As noted previously, this isn't *our* list and this isn't what *we* want to know. This is what funders want. Which means this is the information you should provide in *every* proposal to *every* funder, including those funders that don't provide you with a list of topics to cover or questions to answer. Use this as your blueprint in crafting your proposals.

LIKE BUILDING A HOUSE WITHOUT THE BLUEPRINTS

Unfortunately, either many grantwriters are working without this architectural plan for building successful proposals, or they don't know how to effectively organize their material within the generally prescribed framework. And a disorganized proposal can be fatal.

We asked grantmakers from around the country how frequently they received disorganized proposals and if so, what kind of impression these made. Nearly two-thirds of the respondents reported receiving disorganized proposals "frequently" or "often" and as much as 20 percent to 30 percent of the time. There was near uniformity about what kind of impression a disorganized proposal makes: not good. Here's a sampling of some of the comments we received to our question: *What kind of impression does a disorganized proposal make?*

"It usually will not be funded." (Carolyn Young, Hogg Foundation for Mental Health)

"A bad impression. If we don't have time to do a site visit to compensate for a bad proposal, the applicant is out of luck." (David Steven Rappoport, Maine Health Access Foundation)

"It raises a red flag about the ability of the organization to carry out the project." (Denise San Antonio Zeman, St. Luke's Foundation of Cleveland, Ohio)

"Very bad. A disorganized proposal makes it very difficult for my 24 readers to follow along in meetings or on conference calls when judging many proposals at once." (Pam LeRose, West Virginia Humanities Council)

"The impression that the applicant is a disorganized organization. However, the most organized proposal doesn't necessarily mean an organized or sophisticated organization." (Andrea L. Reynolds, Community Foundation of Greater Memphis)

Even though there was near uniformity among survey respondents that disorganized proposals leave a negative impression, there were a couple of dissenting voices. Barbara Silzle of the Leeway Foundation says that the impression presented by a disorganized proposal is of "no real relevance." She continues, "We try very hard to listen for the content, not the format."

And Allen Smart of the Rapides Foundation finds disorganized proposals "more distracting than anything else."

Nevertheless, it is clear that disorganized proposals strike a nerve with the vast majority of funders. Let's take a look at an example of a truly disorganized proposal, an "ugly duckling."

Knitting for Nippers
Proposal to the Gregory Norwood Family Foundation

History and Mission of Knitting for Nippers

Knitting for Nippers was founded in 1991 by Pearl Thisaway in the Riverview Park Neighborhood of Metropolitan City for low-income and economically disadvantaged youth-at-risk to give them an alternative to negative influences in their lives, such as gang activity, drugs, and other risky behaviors. Pearl herself grew up in the impoverished neighborhood and is knowledgeable about the hard choices facing young lives. Pearl received an education, spent her adult life as a successful businesswoman in England, then returned to the community where she was raised and took an early retirement. Throughout her life, she always knitted, having been taught by her grandmother. Pearl began teaching neighborhood children in 1989 and immediately saw that knitting gave them the lifelong skills of focus and discipline and the personal satisfaction that comes from achieving realistic goals. The first children she taught—in her own living room—were third graders from the Betsy Ross Elementary School. Their first project was a cobalt blue scarf.

Soon Pearl was invited by the Betsy Ross Elementary School principal to teach knitting as an after-school enrichment program for children of all grades (K through 5). Enrollment soared. Pearl had more students than she could supervise so she hired high school interns to assist her. Within two years, more than half of the children enrolled at the Betsy Ross Elementary School were taking, or had taken, knitting classes, including 35% of the boys. Knitting sessions last eight weeks and coincide with other enrichment offerings, such as sports and music programs. Four sessions of eight weeks are offered during the regular school year. The program hires only experienced knitters who have previously worked with children and youth. Many of the program's high school interns have previously been students themselves in Knitting for Nippers. All instructors are required to attend a rigorous 30-day training program that helps prepare them for the challenges of teaching knitting in an after-school setting.

Because the majority of Knitting for Nippers ("Nippers") students qualifies for the school district's free lunch program, we provide a nutritious after school snack, such as raisins, carrots or fruit wraps, so they maintain their energy during the lessons. The program also offers children bottled water. Please note that Nippers does not provide sugar snacks or soft drinks to participants.

Since other elementary and middle schools serving low-income populations in the Metropolitan City School District began taking an interest in the Nippers program, we increased the number of participating schools between 1991 and 1996 from one school to 11 schools. However, because the financially strapped School District could not afford the program costs, especially at so many new schools, Pearl realized that she would need to raise philanthropic contributions if she was going to offer her exceptional program at more schools. Program costs include stipends for the high school interns, yarn and needles, plus the snacks provided to participating students.

Knitting for Nippers ("Nippers") was incorporated as a 501(c)(3) not-for-profit organization in 1991 with a board of directors of three dedicated members of the community: Pearl Thisaway (program founder and first Executive Director), Carmela Sanchez (a child psychologist) and Nancy Drew (a noted private investigator). Our motto has always been "A Stitch in Time," for the early intervention with youth at-risk will help keep them away from negative influences.

Since then, Nippers has grown tremendously. Today, the program is offered in 18 elementary and middle schools serving ethnically diverse, low-income populations in the Metropolitan City School District and reaches approximately 12,000 students annually during the regular school year. An additional 1,500 students participate in the SummerFun Knitting Program that is offered in conjunction with the Metropolitan Park District's summer program. Nippers has also sprouted sister programs in five other cities around the country: Boston, Tampa, New Orleans, Chicago, and our newest program in Phoenix. These sister programs use the Nippers template, but are separate 501(c)(3) nonprofit agencies in their respective states. Recently, the Nippers' staff, which now totals four full-time and two part-time employees, has been having discussions with the Metropolitan City Police Department about piloting a knitting program for youth who are incarcerated in the juvenile justice system as it is well-documented that knitting is a relaxing activity and can be used as a tool for anger management and conflict resolution.

Nippers has an annual operating budget of $725,000 and a board of directors comprised of 12 community leaders. They have 100% participation in financially supporting the organization. The Nippers board of directors list is one of the attachments attached to this proposal. Full-time staff members include an Executive Director, a Development Director, a Program Director, and an Assistant Program Director. The two part-time staff members are a Volunteer Coordinator and a Finance Manager. Nippers uses contract personnel to provide information technology and bookkeeping support services. Recently, Pearl Thisaway resigned as Executive Director after many years of dedicated service, and Tilly Fisk became the new ED.

Nippers' mission is to provide low-income and economically disadvantaged at-risk youth with a positive alternative to negative influences in their lives, such as gang activity, drugs and other risky behaviors. Participating youth will also learn an important skill that they can use throughout their lives.

"We are proud to offer the Nippers program at our school," says Lionel Lincoln, principal of the Betsy Ross Elementary School. "Our students learn important skills, are encouraged to avoid negative behaviors and above all have great fun."

Knitting for Nippers' Request to the Gregory Norwood Family Foundation

Nippers submits this proposal to the Gregory Norwood Family Foundation requesting unrestricted grant funding of $25,000. Grant funds will support Nippers programs in Metropolitan City elementary and middle schools. Nippers has carefully and methodically reviewed the Foundation's guidelines and believes that we are a good fit under the category of "youth at-risk and crafts." Other recent Nippers funders include the Met City Community Foundation ($50,000), the Champion Fund ($10,000) and Seriously Important Corporation ($7,500). Philanthropic contributions account for about 75% of our total budget of $750,000, or $562,500 of the total. Other sources of revenue include: fees from our summer program (which is not limited to at-risk youth, but draws diverse students from throughout the city); interest from our endowment; and earned income from the sale of scarves, sweaters, potholders and other items knitted by student participants in the program.

As a grantor at the Gold Needles Level, the Foundation will be prominently recognized: (1) on the Nippers Web site; (2) in our newsletter; (3) in our Honor Roll of Donors published in our annual report;

and (4) on a commemorative scarf that will be specially knitted by a student intern and hand delivered to the Foundation.

We hope the Foundation will be interested in investing in Knitting for Nippers. Our motto is "A Stitch in Time" for we believe in the early intervention with youth at-risk who otherwise face many negative influences, such as gang activity, drugs and other risky behaviors. The Gregory Norwood Family Foundation's grant of $25,000 can make a big difference in the life of a young person attending school in Metropolitan City.

Our excellent work has been recognized by many organizations in the community. Nippers received the Metropolitan City's Gold Key Award for Excellence in 1996 and we were designated a "Bright Beacon of Light" by the International Society of Knitting Fanatics in 1998. Our program has been featured in numerous newspaper articles and television shows, including Early Evening Magazine, City Streets, and on the 24-hour Knitting Channel. Pearl Thisaway, the program's founder who now serves as an emeritus member on the board of directors, has also been honored for her pioneering work. She was named Knitter of the Year and received an Outstanding Enrichment Teacher of the Year Award.

The Needs Statement

Youth today face numerous challenges, such as gang activity, drugs, criminal behavior and other risky behaviors. This is especially true for youth living in low-income households and neighborhoods in Metropolitan City, such as Riverview Park, Knobby Knolls and the Tidal Basin. In these communities, there is rampant unemployment (almost 30% according to labor figures released by the city last year). These neighborhoods also post high crime rates and gang activity.

Appallingly, children as young as 8 and 9 years old have been recruited by local gangs. School drop out rates are an alarming 25% higher than the citywide average and truancy rates are equally worrisome, according to a recent school district report. Young people who drop out of school and/or become involved with drugs and/or criminal activity, including gangs, are most likely to be unable to find stable employment at jobs that offer salaries higher than the minimum wage. Therefore, young people in these communities need an alternative.

Without Nippers, the only other healthy option is for youth to participate in after school sports programs, such as those offered at the Tidal Basin Community Center. However, not all young people want to participate in the rigorous athletic program. And, we have found that even a significant number of athletes want to get involved in an activity as relaxing as knitting. In a 2000 study conducted at the Riverview Park Middle School, a full 24.5% of the student body reported "not interested" in playing sports involving a ball. In that same survey, nearly 88% of the reporting students said that knitting "interests me greatly."

No other knitting program is presently offered to these underserved youth. And we have a proven track record of success. Of the 12,000 students who participated in our program last year, 99% remained in school, 55% maintained at least a B average (nearly 90% maintained at least a C average) and less than 5% have entered the juvenile justice system. Furthermore, truancy rates for participating students were significantly less than those for non-participating students. In the coming school year, our goal is to ensure that every student who participants in the Nippers program will remain in school. We also plan to decrease the truancy rate by 15% and increase the number of students who maintain a B average to 75% (with at least 95% of the participating students earning a C or better). Participating children who do not maintain a C average are given another chance because we believe that everyone deserves another chance. Children with below C averages are encouraged to bring their grades up in the following grading period and usually they do.

Nippers also intends to involve local neighborhood foot patrol officers with the program by having them make monthly presentations to the students. Therefore, we anticipate lowering the number of students who enter the juvenile justice system to well under 2.5%.

It is important to remember that Nippers' mission is to provide low-income and economically disadvantaged at-risk youth with a positive alternative to negative influences in their lives like gang activity, drugs and other risky behaviors. Participating youth learn skills they can use throughout their lives.

Program Description

Nippers provides an after school alternative to youth in grades K through 8. We offer the best knitting program for youth in the city. Students, who are assigned to a class based on age and knitting ability, meet three days each week at their respective schools for one hour following the regular school day. The teacher-student ratio averages 1:10. Teachers are generally high school interns who receive a modest stipend of $120 per month for their work. Other instructors are volunteers from the community who work without pay. All instructors, whether interns or volunteers, are required to complete a 30-day intensive training program to better prepare them for the classroom experience. Students are given incentives to encourage them to achieve academically.

In addition to receiving beginning, intermediate and advanced knitting instruction, students are also provided with key life skills training and gain self-esteem. Our youngest students also gain better manual dexterity and improved fine motor skills. The program is flexible and students work at their own pace. While knitting at home or at the movies is encouraged, it is not required. Since Nippers serves a predominantly low-income population, no fees are charged. We provide the yarn and the needles, along with patterns, instruction, healthy snacks and bottled water.

In addition to our regular after school program, we also offer a special summer program in conjunction with the Metropolitan City Parks & Recreation Department. The summer program is offered in two-week modules of half-day duration. Because we offer the summer program at neighborhood parks that have convenient swimming pools, we also provide a 1-hour swimming break during the half-day sessions. The summer program is offered to children ages 5 to 13 years of age. Summer program instructors are generally paid high school interns.

Creativity is encouraged whether youth are attending the regular session or the summer program. On average, a child spends 6.5 years in the Nippers program and will have completed more than 25 different knitting projects during their time with us.

Evaluation of Our Program

Nippers is committed to offering the best knitting program for youth in the city. We conduct ongoing evaluations to help us determine what is and isn't working. Nippers uses both quantitative and qualitative measures. Quantitative measures include tracking: (1) the number of students enrolled at participating schools; (2) the grade point averages of participating students (youth must maintain a "C" average to participate; however one of our objectives is for 75% of our students to maintain a B minus or better average); (3) the number of students who remain in school while enrolled in Nippers; and (4) the number of students who do not enter the juvenile justice system while enrolled in Nippers. Some of this information is challenging to obtain because of privacy issues with the Metropolitan City School District; however, we do our best.

We also ask all instructors to complete a written evaluation at the end of each eight-week session. Their responses help us design the curriculum for the intensive 30-day training program. More than half of our high school interns will return the following year. We lose some students to high school graduation and college, while others resign for better paying part-time jobs. Still, nearly 90% of our interns and volunteer instructors report "high" satisfaction on their written surveys.

"I LOVE working in the Nippers program!" writes Sheila, a 15 year-old high school sophomore who herself spent seven years participating in the Nippers program. "The program has given me terrific skills and job training—things I will need to succeed in life."

Measurable Outcomes

Students usually begin by learning to knit a scarf in a color of their own choosing. Once the student has knitted a scarf for everyone in his or her own immediate family, then they are encouraged to progress to more complicated projects, such as hats, potholders and eventually vests and sweaters. The outcome is for each participating student to complete at least one project during the eight-week session. However, for those projects that take longer than the eight weeks, the student is allowed to carry the project forward to the next session. The summer program, which lasts only two-weeks per session, limits students to scarf-work only, although a few of the more advanced students have also completed potholders during the prescribed period.

Students take great pride in their finished items. Little Angus, a fourth grader and second-year participant, says, "I love my Day-Glo orange scarf and wear it every day! Knitting class is the best time of the day."

Another outcome is the difference the Nippers program makes in the lives of families. We encourage parents to get involved and help their young knitters. Even if they do not themselves knit, parents can encourage the activity by providing a quiet, well lit space at home, and by attending Nippers family events. At the end of each eight-week session, we hold a mini fashion show where students model their creations for family and friends. Awards are presented to the "Most Improved Knitter," "Most Creative Project," and "Most Academically Improved Knitter." The children and families take great pride in their work and these awards.

Future Funding

Knitting for Nippers has been going strong for 15 years, and we are committed to securing our financial future. An unrestricted grant from the Gregory Norwood Family Foundation will help Nippers provide quality knitting instruction for some 12,000 elementary and middle school students in the coming school year. Your grant will help us purchase yarn and needles, as well as provide stipends for our high school interns.

Next year, Nippers plans to form the Pearl Thisaway Society to recognize individual donors of $500 or more. Additionally, we will continue to expand our grantseeking program, as well as hold our first-ever special fundraising event that is expected to raise more than $100,000 for our worthwhile programs. We respectfully ask the Gregory Norwood Family Foundation for a grant of $25,000 and hope you will find our program worthy of your investment.

JUMBLED ORDER

This proposal is a mess. It seems more like a crazy quilt than a knitted scarf. The section order is mixed up. It's difficult to find, much less follow, a logical train of thought. The proposal is riddled with redundancies, one of the common problems with disorganized proposals. And it's too wordy and filled with extraneous details. Let's review these problems in some sort of rational order, which is something the writer didn't do.

Problem Number One

Unlike many disorganized proposals, at least this one has headings to help the reader locate specific information; however, the narrative doesn't follow the standard sequence of proposal components. It begins with History and Mission, followed by the Request, the Needs Statement, Program Description, Evaluation, Measurable Outcomes, and Future Funding. Because this is not in the order funders are accustomed to seeing, the proposal is likely to confuse and frustrate them.

As Karen Topakian of the Agape Foundation explains, "I have to work harder [at reading a disorganized proposal]."

Our job as grantwriters is to make it as easy as possible for program officers to learn about our agency, the problem being addressed, and our agency's strategy for addressing the need. Organize proposals in the "usual order," unless instructed to do otherwise. By doing so, you meet the expectations of the program officer— and your proposal is easy to follow.

Problem Number Two

Not only are the sections in this proposal out of order, but the content within the respective sections is illogical. Each section includes information that really belongs in another section. The author seems to be writing from a stream of consciousness rather than following a logical flow. For example, in the History and Mission section, the writer begins by recounting (perhaps in too much detail) how Knitting for Nippers was founded. By the end of the second paragraph, the writer slides into a description of the program with the sentence, "The program hires only experienced knitters who have previously worked with children and youth."

In the third paragraph, the proposal delves further into extremely minute program details concerning the fact that nutritious snacks will be served to participating children. This information about nutritious snacks has no business being included in the History and Mission section. Furthermore, it probably does not even belong in the Methods section. This info is minutia, and it does not advance the agency's case for support. This tidbit should be left on the cutting-room floor.

Problem Number Three

This proposal is chock-full of redundancies. For example, the agency's mission is repeated twice, the first time near the end of the History and Mission section and the second time at the conclusion of the Needs Statement. The Nippers' famous motto, "A Stitch in Time," is also repeated twice: in the History section and in the Request section. The statement, "We offer the best knitting program for youth in the city," which appears in the Program Description, is echoed in the Evaluation section with "Nippers is committed to offering the best knitting program for youth in the city."

Redundancies are a problem for two reasons. First, something said the first time has impact. In the Nippers' proposal, there's the agency's mission. Its motto or tag line. Its stated commitment to excellence. Each statement is important and deserves attention. However, their impact is diluted with each repeating. It's as if the agency has to keep repeating its message in order to make it true. The second problem is that redundancies are like speed bumps in an otherwise flowing story. They slow the reader down as she pauses to ask herself, Haven't I read this before?

Problem Number Four

This ugly duckling proposal also suffers from a terminal case of florid writing (which is covered in Chapter Eight) and the inclusion of too many irrelevant details. Evidence of these twin maladies can be found in the proposal's opening paragraph, with the revelation that the first knitting project for that initial group of third graders was "a cobalt blue scarf." That colorful bit of info (pun intended) is more detail than any funder could possibly need or want.

Here's a roundup of a few of the other irrelevancies found in this proposal:

- "We provide a nutritious after school snack, such as raisins, carrots or fruit wraps" as found in the History and Mission section.
- The string listing of staff titles, Executive Director, Development Director, Program Director, Assistant Program Director, Volunteer Coordinator, and Finance Manager, in the History and Mission section.
- "We provide the yarn and needles, along with patterns, instruction, healthy snacks and bottled water" from the Program Description.
- Much of the Measurable Outcomes section.

We want to emphasize that not all details are irrelevant or superfluous. Selected, relevant details can breathe life into a proposal. For example, the background information about Nippers' founder, Pearl Thisaway, is rich with relevant details, particularly the fact that she grew up in the same impoverished neighborhood first served by the Nippers program and that she became a successful businesswoman in her adult life. This shows why she has a strong commitment to the community and its youth. Similarly important are the details regarding the interns who provide program instruction. It is a positive reflection on the program that former participants frequently return to assume new roles as instructors.

In conclusion, a successful proposal writer chooses which details to include with an eye toward which ones will further the case for support. All others are superfluous and are better left behind.

WHAT WENT WRONG

We can speculate as to the reasons why this proposal is such a disorganized mess. Perhaps it was written by an inexperienced grantwriter. Perhaps the writer avoided using an outline to help organize and arrange his or her thoughts. Or perhaps it was hurriedly cobbled together to meet a deadline, with the writer cutting and pasting copy here and there from several different proposals to assemble this one.

Ultimately, it probably doesn't make a difference as to why the proposal is in such disarray. In this highly competitive grantseeking environment, funders generally cannot distinguish proposals written by novice grantwriters from those cobbled together by seasoned professionals—and the vast majority of disorganized proposals will earn the program officer's scorn. Yet some program officers will give an applicant the benefit of the doubt, especially when the applicant is a grassroots agency.

Dolores E. Roybal of the Santa Fe Community Foundation says the impression made by disorganized proposals is "generally poor," but she adds, "we have made some exceptions for small, grassroots organizations."

"Usually, [a disorganized proposal] indicates a grassroots organization and that perhaps they should be adding a small capacity portion to the grant," says Judith Murphy, Y&H Soda Foundation. "A phone call usually helps to clarify but if not then I wonder how much they really understand what they are doing."

Judith L. Woodruff of the Northwest Health Foundation is willing to go even further, saying, "The most immediate response is doubt that the project can succeed if they can't get an organized proposal together. It means that we need to intervene with the organization and offer technical assistance funds or consultants to help them develop the proposal more fully."

In the previous ugly duckling example, we know the fictitious Knitting for Nippers is no longer a grassroots organization and probably should not require technical assistance. The agency has been in existence for more than fifteen years, it has an annual operating budget of $750,000, and it employs a full-time development director. At this point in the agency's organizational life, Nippers should know better—and produce a better proposal.

THE LAST-MINUTE CUT-AND-PASTE JOB

If a disorganized proposal is the result of a last-minute cut-and-paste job, the funder isn't likely to know or be sympathetic even if they do know.

When a disorganized proposal comes across Liesel Fenner's (New England Foundation for the Arts) desk, she says, "I will remember that organization and its reputation can become tainted. Moreover, then I have to take the time to give feedback on why the proposal was so poor. Funders often share this info between each other. A poor proposal is not good in the long-term for the organization."

Elizabeth M. Lynch of the Massachusetts Bar Foundation has this to say: "It [a disorganized proposal] can cause a foundation to question whether the organization has a clear goal and plan for the project proposed. It takes extra work on the behalf of the reviewer to ensure that he/she understands both what the project is and to confirm that the applicant is clear on this as well. *There are also instances when it is clear that a proposal was thrown together the night before in order to meet a deadline.* It's important to remember to review the project carefully in these situations because while lack of planning is not a promising start for a proposal, there may be an important project included that a funder might find of interest."

What we're about to say may be totally contrary to the standard operating procedures in many nonprofits. Instead of trying to make every grantmaker deadline, which too often results in hastily prepared proposals, we suggest taking a little more time to do it right—and meeting the next deadline. This is totally reasonable when submitting to funders that have rolling or periodic deadlines. You may need to reconsider this strategy if a targeted funder only has one annual deadline.

> **GRANTWRITING TIP!**
> First impressions are important. This is particularly true with the grantor-grantee relationship. Make sure your proposal doesn't look as if it was stitched together the night before a deadline or prepared by someone without proper experience.

To avoid a last-minute rush to meet a submission deadline, our advice is to plan ahead. There are several steps you can take to help ensure timely and well-prepared submissions:

- Prepare an annual grants calendar and circle the due dates—in red ink if necessary!
- Circulate this grants calendar to other staff members, the board of directors, and the fundraising committee, so scheduling conflicts can be avoided.
- Make your own fictitious "early-bird" deadlines at least a week or two (three or four is even better!) before the funder's real deadlines—and stick with yours.
- Give other agency staff members (for example, program directors, finance manager, accountant, and the like) sufficient warning if you'll be needing them to provide you with information for a grant application. An early heads-up is most appreciated.

- Consider waiting until the grantmaker's next funding cycle if caught in a time squeeze.

POSITIVE COMMENTS FOR THE NIPPERS PROPOSAL

Having identified the many major flaws in the Nippers proposal, we want to note what is good about it.

One of the first positive items to jump out is the fact that the proposal uses headings. Granted, they are in a jumbled order, but at least some attempt was made to provide an organizational structure. We're huge fans of headings. When properly ordered, headings provide proposals with a structure. They serve as signposts for the reader, guiding them to what information is covered in a particular section.

A second positive is the inclusion of quotes. If relevant and not overdone, client quotes can enliven a proposal narrative. But we caution that irrelevant quotes or too many of them can have the opposite effect. It's the law of diminishing returns. We talk more about quotes, as well as client stories, in Chapter Three. What funders have to say may surprise you.

Finally, despite all of its flaws, this proposal can be informative and entertaining. Even though the reader must wade through a lot of irrelevant details that are presented in a haphazard fashion, the core information is all there. After reading through to the end, the reader will know something about Nippers' history, mission, the problem it is trying to address in specific neighborhoods of Metropolitan City, the clients being served, how Nippers measures its success, and how it plans to fund its work in the future.

REMIX: GIVING ORDER TO THE DISORDER

Fixing a disorganized proposal is one of the more challenging tasks in grantwriting. Consider it a major remodel. As mentioned earlier, allowing enough time to write and working from an outline can help reduce the incidence of disorganized proposals.

Let's see if we can bring some order to the chaos of the Nippers proposal. Here's the "beautiful swan" rewrite:

Knitting for Nippers
Proposal to the Gregory Norwood Family Foundation

Knitting and Much More: the History and Mission of Knitting for Nippers

Knitting for Nippers ("Nippers") is a 501(c)(3) not-for-profit organization founded in 1991. What started in a living room as a knitting class for a handful of third graders has grown into a flourishing after-school enrichment program that annually reaches 12,000 students in 18 elementary and middle schools in the Metropolitan City School District (MCSD). Pearl Thisaway, a successful businesswoman who grew up in the impoverished Riverview Park neighborhood and returned there in her retirement, conceived of the program and taught the first class. She had a vision that knitting lessons could provide low-income youth who are at risk of truancy, dropping out of school, joining gangs, and engaging in criminal behavior with a life-enriching alternative. Word spread of her in-home class, and soon Pearl was invited by the neighborhood elementary school principal to teach knitting as an after-school enrichment program for children in grades K through 5. Enrollment soared at the Betsy Ross Elementary School. Soon Pearl was hiring high school interns to assist her. The program kept expanding. Between 1991 and 1996, the number of participating schools increased to 11 and 7 more have been added since then.

In 1997, Nippers began offering summer classes through the Metropolitan Park District. Last year, approximately 1,500 students participated in the SummerFun Knitting Program. Recently, Nippers staff initiated discussions with the Metropolitan City Police Department about piloting a knitting program for youth who are incarcerated in the juvenile justice system. They recognize that knitting is a relaxing activity that can be used as a tool for anger management and conflict resolution. Nippers has also sprouted sister programs in five cities across the country: Boston, Tampa, New Orleans, Chicago, and Phoenix. These programs, which use the Nippers template, are independent nonprofit agencies.

Nippers has an annual operating budget of $725,000. The agency is staffed by four full-time and two part-time employees and is governed by a 12-member board of directors. After more than a dozen years of dedicated service, Pearl Thisaway retired as Executive Director in 2003 and now holds the title of Executive Director Emeritus. Tilly Fisk is the current Executive Director. She joined the agency in 2003, having previously worked as deputy director of a non-profit agency that provides tutoring for middle school youth and as an elementary school teacher.

Over the years, Nippers' excellence has been recognized by many organizations in the community. In 1996, Nippers received the Metropolitan City's Gold Key Award for Excellence, and in 1998, Nippers was designated a "Bright Beacon of Light" by the International Society of Knitting Fanatics. The program has been featured in numerous newspaper articles and television shows, including Early Evening Magazine, City Streets, and the 24-hour Knitting Channel.

The Needs Statement: "A Stitch in Time"

The Nippers' motto is "A Stitch in Time," for the agency was founded on the belief that early intervention with at-risk youth can offset negative influences such as gang involvement, drugs, and criminal activity. Youth today face numerous challenges. Appallingly, children as young as 8 and 9 years old have been recruited by local gangs. Young people living in low-income households and neighborhoods in Metropolitan City, such as Riverview Park, Knobby Knolls, and the Tidal Basin, are especially vulnerable. In these communities, there is rampant unemployment (almost 30% according to statistics released by the city last year in *Employment and Unemployment in Metropolitan City: A Report*). These neighborhoods also post high crime rates and gang activity. School drop-out rates are an alarming 25% higher than the citywide average, and truancy rates are equally worrisome (*What's Happening in Our Schools*, a report published by the Metropolitan City School District, 2005).

Young people who drop out of school and/or become involved with drugs and/or criminal activity, including gangs, are most likely to be unable to find stable employment at jobs that offer salaries higher than the minimum wage. Although experimenting with this behavior is usually more likely among high school students, negative influences begin early, often in elementary and middle school. Therefore, young people in the Riverview Park, Knobby Knolls, and Tidal Basin neighborhoods need an alternative.

Without Nippers, the only other option is for youth to participate in after-school sports programs, such as those offered at the Tidal Basin Community Center. However, not all young people want to participate in a rigorous athletic program. Furthermore, many young athletes have expressed a desire to want to get involved with an alternative activity, such as knitting. In fact, in a 2000 study conducted at the Riverview Park Middle School, nearly 25% of the student body of 750 students reported "not interested" in playing ball sports. In that same survey, nearly 88% of the respondents said that "knitting interests me greatly." Despite this keen interest in knitting among Metropolitan City youth, Nippers is the only knitting program offered to elementary and middle school children.

Since 1991, Nippers has given youth in grades K through 8 an opportunity to learn to knit, a positive alternative to risky and possibly dangerous behaviors. Community support from foundations and corporations will enable the Nippers program to continue.

Measurable Outcomes: Nippers Participants Will Make the Grades

"I love my Day-Glo orange scarf and wear it every day! Knitting class is the best time of the day," says Angus, a fourth grader at the Tidal Basin Elementary School.

Nippers is committed to being more than just a knitting program and strives to give low-income, at-risk youth the tools they will need for success throughout life: discipline, patience, perseverance, commitment, and pride of accomplishment. In addition, younger children develop their manual dexterity and fine motor skills.

Of the 12,000 students who participated in the Nippers after-school program last year, 99% remained in school, 55% maintained at least a B average, nearly 90% maintained at least a C average, and less than 5% entered the juvenile justice system. Furthermore, truancy rates for participating students were significantly less than those for nonparticipating students. In the coming academic year, with an estimated 12,200 participating students, the goal is to ensure that every participating student will remain in school. Additional measurable outcomes are the following:

- Decrease the truancy rate by 15%
- Increase the number of participants who maintain at least a B average from 55% to 75%
- Increase the number of participants who maintain at least a C average from nearly 90% to at least 95%

- Decrease the number of participants who enter the juvenile justice system from less than 5% to less than 2.5%

One final outcome, much less amenable to measurable outcomes, is the difference the program makes in the lives of individual families. Nippers encourages parents to get involved and help their young knitters. Even if parents do not knit, they can support their children by providing them with a quiet, well-lit space at home. In addition, they can attend the mini-fashion show at the end of each session, as well as other Nippers events.

Program Description:
Methods for Success

In the last academic year, 12,000 students participated free of charge in the Nippers program at 18 elementary and middle schools. (MCSD provides Nippers with the classroom space rent free, thereby helping to keep Nippers costs down.) In the coming school year, Nippers anticipates serving the same 18 schools while increasing the number of participating students to 12,200. Classes will meet three days a week at their respective schools for one hour following the regular school day. Sessions are eight weeks long and there are four sessions per year. Because Nippers serves a predominantly low-income population, classes are free, and all materials, such as yarn, needles, patterns, and instructions, are provided. In addition, healthy snacks and bottled water are available to the students.

Classes are taught by either volunteers or high school interns, who receive a modest stipend of $120 per month. All instructors are experienced knitters who must complete a 30-day intensive training program to prepare them for the classroom experience. A majority of the interns are former participants of the Nippers program. The student-teacher ratio is 10:1. In addition to providing knitting instruction, teachers also offer help and encouragement to the students regarding their homework and academic studies. Participating students are encouraged to maintain at least a C average and are given incentives ("rewards," such as trinkets and candy) for earning top grades on assignments and report cards. However, no student is ever denied access to the program due to academic problems.

In the approaching school year, Nippers will strengthen the academic component of its program by extending each daily session from 1 hour to 1½ hours. The additional half hour will be devoted to homework or silent reading, and children may also seek specific help from their teacher. Nippers will also strengthen that aspect of the program that seeks to deter risky behavior. Nippers is working with the Metropolitan City Police Department and hopes to engage local neighborhood foot patrol officers in making monthly presentations to the participating students.

Students are assigned to a class based on their age and knitting ability. Beginning students usually start by knitting a scarf in a color of their own choosing. Once students have knitted a scarf for every member of their immediate family, they are encouraged to progress to more complicated projects, such as hats, pot holders, and eventually vests and sweaters. Each student is expected to complete at least one project during the eight-week session. Creativity is highly encouraged. At the conclusion of each eight-week session, each school holds a mini-fashion show, where students model their creations for invited family and friends. Awards are also presented to the "Most Improved Knitter," "Most Creative Project," and "Most Academically Improved Knitter."

On average, a child will spend 6.5 years in the Nippers program and will have completed more than 25 different knitting projects during this time. The program's popularity is evident, as 97.5% of the students elect to continue in the subsequent session.

In addition to the regular after-school program, Nippers offers a summer program in conjunction with the Metropolitan City Parks & Recreation Department. The SummerFun Knitting Program is held at neighborhood parks, combining a half day of swimming and knitting in two-week modules. Last summer, 1,500 students in grades K through 8 participated in SummerFun.

How Nippers Will Evaluate Program Effectiveness

Nippers conducts ongoing evaluation to determine what is and isn't working and uses both quantitative and qualitative measures. Quantitative measures include tracking (1) the number of students enrolled at participating schools; (2) the number of projects completed by each student and by the entire enrollment; (3) the grade point averages of participating students; (4) the truancy rate for students who are in the program; and (5) the number of students who do not enter the juvenile justice system while enrolled in Nippers.

All instructors are asked to complete a written evaluation form at the end of each eight-week session. Their candid responses are used to help design improvements to the curriculum for the intensive 30-day training program. More than 90% of the teachers report "high" satisfaction. While some high school interns leave the program due to graduation or better paying jobs, more than half return each year. Sheila, a recent returning student intern and seven-year Nippers participant, wrote, "I LOVE working in the Nippers program! The program has given me terrific skills and job training—things I will need to succeed in life."

Future Funding to Ensure Nippers Sustainability

Nippers has been going strong for 15 years, and the organization is committed to securing its financial future. Philanthropic contributions from foundations, corporations, and individuals account for about 75% of the Nippers $725,000 annual budget, or $562,500. Other sources of revenue include fees from the SummerFun program (as this program is not limited to low-income, at-risk youth but enrolls economically diverse students from throughout the city), interest earned from the endowment fund, and earned income from the sale of scarves, sweaters, and other items that are knitted by student participants and sold on the Nippers Web site. Grants will continue to be a major source of Nippers funding in the future. In addition, next year Nippers plans to establish the Pearl Thisaway Society, a donor recognition society, as a means to encourage more gifts of $500 and more from individuals. Nippers intends to raise an additional $20,000 in major gifts through the Pearl Thisaway Society. Finally, Nippers plans to hold its first-ever fundraising event in the coming year, with the goal of raising more than $100,000 to support Nippers programs.

Nippers' Request to the Gregory Norwood Family Foundation

Knitting for Nippers is a marvelous program that helps meet the needs of youth living in some of the most troubled neighborhoods in Metropolitan City. An unrestricted grant of $25,000 from the Gregory Norwood Family Foundation will enable Nippers to continue to provide quality knitting instruction to 12,200 elementary and middle school students in the upcoming school year. This grant will help purchase yarn, knitting needles, and snacks, as well as provide modest stipends for high school interns. Nippers hopes that the Foundation will find this program worthy of investment.

DISORGANIZED PROPOSAL MAKEOVER: A SOLID STRUCTURE

The puzzle pieces fit together better in this version. The sections have been reorganized so they follow the more standard proposal format: History and Mission, Needs Statement, Measurable Outcomes, Program Description, Methods, Evaluation, Future Funding, and the formal Request for Funding.

In addition to reordering the sections, the material within those sections has been reordered.

Compare the two History and Mission sections. The "ugly duckling" version takes up nearly two full 8½-by-11 pages and is filled with information that belongs either elsewhere in the proposal or nowhere in the proposal. For example, the list of staff job titles can be jettisoned from the narrative, for it is extraneous to most funders. Should a grantmaker want such information, generally they will request an organizational chart or a budget that itemizes each position.

Also deleted in this version are the names of the founding board of directors, which are irrelevant. Detailed program information has been moved to that section and several sentences have been compressed, making them sharper. What had been two pages now comfortably fits on one 8½-by-11 sheet.

Another improvement is moving the Request section to the end of the proposal rather than having it float somewhere in the middle of the narrative. Your agency's formal request, enhanced by a sentence or two that summarize the program, is a tidy conclusion to any proposal.

WRITING BILLBOARD HEADINGS

One of the other major improvements found in the beautiful swan version concerns the section headings. As noted earlier in the chapter, headings serve an important function in a proposal. Like street signs, they inform readers where they are. For example, under the heading Future Funding, you expect what follows to be information about how the agency plans to fund the program after the grant period expires. It is certainly acceptable to use simple terms as section headings, such as Needs Statement, Goals and Objectives, and Methods, but a savvy writer will get a little more creative—and persuasive.

In the revised proposal, notice that History and Mission of Knitting for Nippers has been transformed to Knitting and Much More: The History and Mission of Knitting for Nippers. The addition of "and Much More" imparts some crucial information to the reader. It says that the agency provides more than just knitting instruction. Similarly, The Needs Statement is now The Needs Statement: A Stitch in Time, which showcases the double meaning of the agency's motto or tag line, and Measurable Outcomes has been expanded to Measurable Outcomes: Nippers Participants Will Make the Grades.

Each of these headings retains its street sign function by retaining key words, such as *History and Mission, Needs Statement,* and *Measurable Outcomes.* But the revised headings also serve as advertising billboards, persuasively presenting your message in bold letters. We want to emphasize that not every heading needs to be given the neon-light treatment. Rather, headings serve an important function in a grant proposal (street signs), and you should at least consider whether or not to expand their role to also serve as advertising copy.

WRAPPING UP: DISORGANIZED DISASTERS

Here are some of the one-word responses given by program officers to this survey question: *What kind of impression does a disorganized proposal make?*

"Negative." (Barbara Kemmis, Crossroads Fund)

"Bad." (Christine Elbel, Fleishhacker Foundation; Lynne Rumball, The Greater Tacoma Community Foundation; Barbara Jacobs, Plough Foundation)

"Unprofessional." (Diane Ford, Sobrato Foundation)

"Poor." (M. Carlota Baca, New Mexico Association of Grantmakers)

As the saying goes, you only have one chance to make a first impression. Make sure your grant proposals make a positive, professional first impression with the grantmakers by being well written *and well organized.* Potential funding is riding on it.

The Case of the Missing Needs Statement

Honing the Heart of the Proposal

When we teach proposal writing, we always stress that the Needs Statement—sometimes called the Problem Statement—is the heart of the proposal. When you apply for a grant, you must use the written word to "make the case" to the reader. The Needs Statement can make or break your case.

The need section of the proposal is also the place where you can pique readers' interest by laying out an interesting scenario or describing an intriguing opportunity, arouse their sympathy by helping them picture your clients and the hardships they face, or raise their indignation or sense of justice with an alarming statistic. The goal is to grab readers, convince them of the significance of the issue you are addressing, and persuade them to give serious attention to the rest of your proposal.

In our opinion, this may be the most important part of the proposal, because if you fail here, you are not likely to be successful in attracting funds for your work. In our survey of grantmakers, Nora Maloy of the Blue Cross Blue Shield of Michigan Foundation agrees, commenting, "I think the Needs Statement is of particular importance in developing a proposal. What problem is the proposal addressing? Is there a gap?"

Accordingly, we usually advise that the Needs Statement is likely to be the longest section of the proposal. For example, in a five-page proposal, laying out the need might take as much as one page or even a bit more, particularly if the problem you are addressing is a new one or one that may be unfamiliar to the grantmaker.

THE NEEDS STATEMENT: IMPORTANCE FOR GRANTMAKERS?

Perhaps we're overly sensitive to the importance of the Needs Statement because as consultants we've seen too many proposals (usually prepared by people new to writing grant proposals) that fail to spell out the need for the project or program they are proposing. But what about the people that really count—the program officers or trustees who will be reviewing your proposals? How often do they see this flaw? In our survey of grantmakers, we asked how often proposal writers assume readers already know the need. Their answers range all across the board, from "almost never" to "frequently"; from one out of ten proposals to 30 percent of the time. Some grantmakers who indicate that they see this infrequently also point out that their guidelines, application form, or process make it very clear what applicants should include to demonstrate the need for their work.

Regardless of how frequently they notice this omission, does a missing or weak Needs Statement lead to a negative decision on funding? Grantmaker opinions vary. To our survey question, "What kind of an impression does it make when the Needs Statement is weak or missing?" most grantmakers respond that it makes a poor impression. According to Andrea L. Reynolds of the Community Foundation of Memphis, "If the 'Needs Section' is weak, the impression made is that the applicant isn't familiar with or knowledgeable about the need. [This] would cause me to wonder if they have the capacity to run the program or project proposed to fit that need." Anne Vally of The James Irvine Foundation agrees. "Demonstrating the need for a particular program is important," she says. "Without it, one wonders about the relevance of the work."

But don't those reviewing proposals already know what the need is? They read enough proposals that one would think they would become experts themselves. Several of those responding to our survey indeed point out that they are already very knowledgeable about the needs in their local community and in the subject areas they fund. As Sandra Sinclair of the J. W. McConnell Foundation says, "It's annoying when they give us a long song and dance about a widespread need as if they are talking to uninformed people. We are professionals and generally well-informed—we have a pretty good idea of the problems that arise, for instance, from homelessness; we don't want to wade through a dissertation—especially at the initial stage. . . . We don't want to be preached at or lectured."

Aaron Jacobs of Social Venture Partners Seattle agrees. He says, "We tell them they should assume we have a handle on the basic needs of populations in our issue areas in our geographic limits. They should establish a need, but don't need to spend more than one of eight pages doing so."

So how does the conscientious proposal writer strike a balance between assuming that the need is known to all and offending a grantmaker by stating the obvious? One solution is to know your grantmaker. Be thorough in your research when you are identifying prospective funders, and be sure to pay attention to what they say they want to see in the Needs Statement. (For more about identifying foundations, see Chapter One, "Demonstrating the Fit.") If the funder is not specific, you should ask. Several of the grantmakers responding to our survey make this point. As Elizabeth M. Lynch of the Massachusetts Bar Foundation says, "We strongly encourage applicants to contact our staff prior to submission, especially when they are new to the proposal process."

In addition, it's not necessary to overwhelm the reader with every piece of information that demonstrates your case, and you should never talk down to your reader. Dave Beckwith of The Needmor Fund says, "If [the need] is missing, [it's] very bad. . . . [but it is] more often overdone with statistics."

Remember that even if grantmakers are experts in the field in which you work, they want to know that you are, too. A strong case statement is one that uses a few well-chosen facts to demonstrate that you have a good grasp of the field and the current situation. As Grace Caliendo of John Muir/Mt. Diablo Community Health Fund puts it, "We tell people 'pretend we don't know; tell us.'" And Carole M. Watson of United Way of the Bay Area adds, "The Needs Section provides the case for the program that is presented to address the needs. Perceiving that we know this information is not an appropriate rationale for 'skating' through this section."

Also, it pays to remember that program officers are often not the decision makers. They may offer recommendations to the trustees or other decision makers, but they won't do your homework for you. You must provide the data that they will use to make their presentation. Mary Gregory of Pacific Foundation Services points out, "It's important because it helps me make the case to the foundation board about why the program is critical." Judith L. Woodruff of the Northwest Health Foundation comments, "I remind people that we have new reviewers and need the background every time."

Let's take a look at a proposal that assumes the reader already understands the need. The following proposal for a homeless resource center in a low-income community demonstrates the flaws of assuming the reader understands the problems to be addressed by the proposed center.

Partnership for Progress—A Collaborative Proposal to the Roberta Gonzalez Foundation for a Homeless Resource Center in Argus County

Introduction and Needs Assessment

In 2005, the Pleasantville Interfaith Alliance, County Social Services and Crisis Intervention, Ella Hogans Community Resources, Inc., and other local agencies participated in a planning process to create a continuum of care for homeless individuals in Argus County. The partnership they planned, Partnership for Progress, is a comprehensive and systematic approach to solving the problem of homelessness in our community and addresses three critical needs: emergency linkage to housing and services through a one-stop Homeless Resource Center; economic and social self-sufficiency through life skills and employment training; and finally, the development of affordable supportive housing.

Partnership for Progress is a thoughtful and carefully considered approach to solving the needs of the homeless in the Argus County community. The funds requested in this proposal to the Argus County Community Fund would provide the core support needed to begin implementation of one component of Partnership for Progress, the one-stop Homeless Resource Center.

According to the Urban Institute, 3.5 million people, 1.35 million of them children, are likely to experience homelessness in the United States in a given year. High unemployment and a depressed economy make Argus County one of the poorest areas in the state. The poverty of Argus County and the lack of a resource center clearly demonstrate the need for a Homeless Resource Center in our community.

Goals and Objectives

The goal of the Homeless Resource Center is to help homeless Argus County families stabilize their lives so that they can find permanent solutions to their housing needs. Objectives to be achieved by the Resource Center are as follows:

- 400 individuals will be linked with temporary housing and other services in the first year.
- 102 will find transitional or permanent housing in the first year.
- Out of 102 individuals who find transitional or permanent housing through the program, 70% (71) will remain in permanent housing for one full year.

Methodology

The Partnership for Progress task force has planned the Homeless Resource Center with an array of services for homeless families and children designed to help them break out of the cycle of homelessness. The Pleasantville Interfaith Alliance will serve as the fiscal agent for this collaborative project.

Services to be provided at the Resource Center are:

- Showers and laundry
- Mail, e-mail and phone service
- Employment services including vocational assessments and training, job counseling, referrals
- Housing assessments, referrals, placements and counseling
- Health screening and referrals and mental health services
- Childcare services
- Transportation subsidies

- Counseling and referrals for social services
- Life skills training
- Money management/representative payee services
- Peer counseling and support groups

These services are meant to help homeless individuals and families stabilize their lives, deal with the issues that led to their homelessness and develop the skills and resources to locate and maintain affordable housing. The program is planned as a "partnership" between the homeless participants and Partnership for Progress. Participants will co-sign agreements that state how they will use the program's resources to achieve greater self-sufficiency. Case managers will assist each participant with the development and maintenance of the plan and organization of the resources. Money management services will help those most unable to function by ensuring that bills (including rent) are paid.

Evaluation

Using the Pleasantville Interfaith Alliance's database, Partnership for Progress will track the clients who use the services of the Homeless Resource Center. This will include demographic information as well as services provided to each client or client family. Individual case files will document progress toward self-sufficiency goals. We plan to host annual reunion events providing incentives (grocery and other merchant vouchers) to foster use of after-care services and to track the long-term housing stability of clients. Invitations will be mailed to former clients and volunteers from local churches will do follow-up calls to encourage attendance.

> ## Budget
>
> A \$300,000 line item operating budget for the first year of the Homeless Resource Center is attached. Partnership for Progress has already received \$125,000 in government funds (county block grant) and partner agencies have pledged \$56,000 in in-kind services. This includes one part-time case manager from County Social Services, space and equipment from Ella Hogans Community Services, Inc. and substantial volunteer support from member congregations of the Pleasantville Interfaith Alliance. We are requesting \$50,000 from your foundation. These funds will be applied to staff salaries for the Resource Center.

WHAT'S WRONG WITH THIS PICTURE?

It may be hard to spot the flaws in this well-written proposal. The writing flows smoothly and conveys its message clearly. For the most part, the defect is not in the narrative that is present; rather, the proposal falls short in what is left unsaid. Except for the last short paragraph in the introductory section, the Needs Statement is "missing-in-action." It's simply not enough to say, as the writer does at the end of that paragraph, "The poverty of Argus County and the lack of a resource center clearly demonstrate the need for a Homeless Resource Center in our community."

ESTABLISHING THE NEED

What should the writer have included? What are the elements that make up a compelling Needs Statement? Catherine T. O'Brien of the William J. & Dorothy K. O'Neill Foundation gives a good overview of what to include in this section when she writes, "Begin with basic statistics on the issue (for example, 'alcoholism affects 80% of the population, resulting in a cost of \$1 billion in lost work time,' etc.), information from professional sources, then information from the organization's statistics (for example, 'How many customers are on the waiting list?')."

A few, well-chosen statistics are always good components, and 84% of our survey respondents agree. Christine Elbel of the Fleishhacker Foundation notes, "In this era of accountability, some facts and figures stating the overall problem or need are essential. Groups should also have data tracking clients served or other outcomes (tickets sold, etc.)."

But it's important to remember that not just any statistics will do. The writer of the proposal just presented includes a statistic, a figure on the dimensions of homelessness in the United States. But the relevance of a national statistic for most local projects is minimal. Several grantmakers point out the futility of including national statistics for a local program. In this Internet age, it's pretty easy to get statistics specific to a local community, and funders know this. Cited by Aaron Jacobs of Social Venture Partners Seattle as a major irritation when he's reviewing proposals is "misuse of statistics," using national or statewide statistics for local or regional programs. "Get the stats for the area you are talking about!"

Choose carefully the statistics you include and remember that just a few will do. You don't want to bog the reader down with too many. Sandra Sinclair of the J. W. McConnell Family Foundation points out, "Be careful; too much of this can make it deadly to read, without adding any value." (For more about this, see Chapter Four, Too Much of a Good Thing.)

And don't forget to cite the source for any statistic. This can be done in a narrative fashion (for example, "According to U.S. census figures . . .") or in brackets after the statistic (for example, "30% of our target population lives in substandard housing [U.S. Census, 2000]").

Other evidence that will help build your case is any indication of the target community's expressed support for the project. Have community members asked for the services to be provided? Have public officials or experts made statements calling for the program that is proposed? Sixty-five percent of our survey respondents name "expert opinions" as important in Needs Statements.

In the case of a proposed program expansion, are clients being turned away by the current provider? Is there a waiting list? Alice Cottingham of Girl's Best Friend Foundation points out, "I always want to know, 'Who asked for this?'"

Defining the target population in terms of size and demographic characteristics is crucial. Who are the people you want to serve? How many are there? How old are they? What is their income level? Where do they live? What is their ethnicity? What are their common characteristics? How do they exhibit the need you plan to address? It's your job to help the reviewer *see* those you want to serve and *feel* their needs.

CLIENT STORIES AND TESTIMONIALS: THE GREAT DEBATE

One way to convey information about the target population and the need is with a short case history or vignette about a typical client. A client story can make the need come alive for the reader. But be careful here. Although 44 percent checked "stories from and about clients" as elements to include in a compelling Needs Statement, only 26 percent feel that way about client testimonials.

Furthermore, grantmakers hold strong but divergent opinions regarding the use of client stories or testimonials in proposals. Opinions range from the terse "Don't include" (from Barbara Jacobs of the Plough Foundation) to "We love them" (from Elizabeth Lynch of the Massachusetts Bar Foundation). For a closer look at the diversity of opinion, see the sidebar below titled The Pros and Cons of Client Stories and Testimonials. Although some funders welcome client stories to balance purely objective data and statistics, others find them too subjective or emotional. Several think client case histories or testimonials are more appropriate during site visits or in grant reports than in proposals.

THE PROS AND CONS OF CLIENT STORIES AND TESTIMONIALS

When we asked grantmakers about the use of client stories and quotes in proposals, we uncovered some strong and opposing viewpoints. The following quotes demonstrate the range of opinions.

The "Pro" Viewpoint

- "A couple [of] relevant stories and/or quotes are appropriate for the proposal." (Carole M. Watson, United Way of the Bay Area)

- "Usually the need is best expressed through the voice of the client; but those stories need to be believable and compelling." (Linda Appleton, The Health Trust)

- "Testimonials are better-written from the voice of the client. A balance of quantitative and qualitative is better than just one or the other." (Aaron Jacobs, Social Venture Partners Seattle)

- "Those are nice, if they show before and after results. The client/neighborhood was in this condition before and now it's in this condition because of the efforts of the program/organization." (Adeeba Deterville, Citibank Community Relations)

- "Crucial: what has the applicant done before, speak to successes AND challenges. Stories go a long way—what were the accidental outcomes? What did the audience think of the work?" (Liesel Fenner, New England Foundation for the Arts)

- "This engages the heart—and even grant reviewers have hearts. There needs to be a balanced approach appropriate to the proposal." (Virginia Elliott, United Methodist Health Ministry Fund)

- "Always, always, always try to get to the emotional level of a reader first, then fill in with statistics and expertise, and finally the solution." (Judith L. Woodruff, Northwest Health Foundation)

- "Stories are key, e.g., the one kid who goes onto art school because they made art in an after school art program." (Liesel Fenner, New England Foundation for the Arts)

The "Con" Viewpoint

- "No, too subjective." (Jacqueline Young, Langendorf Foundation)

- "Never include client stories or quotes. Quotes from clients or client stories often read as self-serving. Not one organization will include negative quotes or stories from clients." (Michell Speight, Dyson Foundation)

- "Personally, I do not find client stories and quotes to be useful. Almost every program can find compelling and moving stories. More important, for me, is to understand the problem that the organization is trying to address, why this particular approach/ program will have impact, and how the organization will know if it has been successful." (Anne Vally, The James Irvine Foundation)

- "Don't try to make me cry, rather be honest about what your work has accomplished." (Barbara Kemmis, Crossroads Fund)

- "This is always a huge mistake with us. We want to see the evidence base for the project." (David Steven Rappoport, Maine Health Access Foundation)

- "I do not like client stories or quotes since I have read too many pages of italicized testimonials that just say how bad something is or how great the program is." (Sandra Treacy, Stone Foundation)

The "Mixed Review"

- "I like these only when they are very pertinent, respectful, and position the speakers as strong people who have something to contribute to the organization and to the community. I hate when quotes and stories are soppy, present speakers as needy and pathetic, or when one voice is [falsely] used to represent a huge group." (Alice Cottingham, Girl's Best Friend Foundation)

- "These are considered anecdotal and therefore receive less weight than hard data." (Denise San Antonio Zeman, Saint Luke's Foundation of Cleveland, Ohio)

- "Fine if they grab our attention and sharpen the presentation; not fine if they have to carry all the weight." (James R. Posner, Posner-Wallace Foundation)

- "Honesty shines through. Sentimentality grates." (Frances Phillips, Walter and Elise Haas Foundation)

- "Include only a few representative stories, with a phrase or sentence connecting it to the mission/focus of the funder organization." (Sister Janet Burkhart, HM, Sisters of the Humility of Mary)

- "Good, but use a light touch. . . . we are not individual donors who can be swayed by a sob story." (Ann McQueen, Boston Foundation)

- "Brevity is appreciated; remember, you're making the case to me, so I can then make the case to my board. If the client stories and quotes are compelling, then by all means, share them!" (Nancy Wiltsek, Pottruck Scott Foundation)

- "The stories should be genuine and verifiable. The quote or story's voice should match the face or situation." (Randy Okamura, SBC)

As always, knowing your prospective donor and its preferences will help you decide what and how much to include. David Steven Rappoport of the Maine

Health Access Foundation offers this advice: "Larger, professional foundations are head-driven, not heart-driven, and proposals to them should be data-driven. Smaller, family foundations are typically more heart-driven. Know your funder."

Lacking specific information about a funder's preference regarding this type of subjective—and often frankly emotional—element means you will have to steer a middle course here. You can do that by monitoring both the quantity and the quality of the stories, quotes, or testimonials you choose to include. Regarding quantity, certainly it is not wise to include dozens of client stories. And don't rely solely on this anecdotal evidence to build your entire Needs Statement. One or two stories backed up by statistics or other data is a safe bet. In addition, be careful of the emotional content of the stories you do choose. No one likes to be manipulated, and an overblown story or quote appearing to do so would not be a good choice.

> **GRANTWRITING TIP!**
> What to include in a Needs Statement:
> - Local statistics for local organizations
> - Expert opinions
> - Data describing the target population—with sources cited
> - Evidence of official or community support

THE DILEMMA FOR ARTS ORGANIZATIONS

Talking about the need for an arts organization can be daunting. Arts programs and projects don't lend themselves as easily to the "Describe the problem, then propose the solution" style of proposal. What is the *problem* that a museum or performing arts organization addresses? What kind of *statistics, research* or *expert opinions* should you come up with to make your case? Frances Phillips of the Walter and Elise Haas Fund addresses this dilemma when she says, "As someone who reviews proposals in the arts, I sometimes find Needs Statements that are overstated. Our field tends to over-compensate in its anxiety about competing with human services and other grantmaking areas. The problem with the overstatements is that the writers set up the context of a need they cannot possibly address in a significant way and that pushes them to identify outcomes they cannot reasonably measure."

Usually, arts groups are better off talking about the *opportunity* than about the *need*. That is, talk about how the proposed project will enhance community life for its residents and visitors. Describe the quality of the program to be offered. Give evidence (audience feedback and attendance figures from similar offerings) to demonstrate the potential audience for the project.

Liesel Fenner of the New England Foundation for the Arts points out, "What's most important is understanding why the art project is important in the first place. Justifying art for art's sake is next to impossible in today's funding climate. We need to understand why the art project is so important that it MUST be created, how it will benefit the artist and most importantly other people, the larger culture and community. It must have multiple meanings that reach others (especially non-arts audiences)."

For a good example of a proposal for an arts organization and project, see Chapter Eight on florid writing.

REVAMPED PROPOSAL: ADDING THE MISSING INGREDIENT

Keep in mind, it's not necessary to include *all* of the suggested elements for a Needs Statement—statistics, expert opinions, target population description, evidence of local support—in *every* proposal. Just choose the ones that make the most sense for your project.

Now that we know what kinds of information to include in a Needs Statement, let's revisit the first part of the flawed Partnership for Progress proposal we started with and see how it can be improved.

Partnership for Progress—A Collaborative
Proposal to the Roberta Gonzalez Foundation
for a Homeless Resource Center in Argus County

Introduction

In 2005, the Pleasantville Interfaith Alliance, County Social Services and Crisis Intervention, Ella Hogans Community Services, Inc., and other local agencies participated in a planning process to create a continuum of care for homeless individuals in Argus County. The partnership they planned, Partnership for Progress, is a comprehensive and systematic plan for solving the problem of homelessness in our community and addresses three critical needs: emergency linkage to housing and services through a one-stop Homeless Resource Center; economic and social self-sufficiency through life skills and employment training; and finally, the development of affordable supportive housing.

Partnership for Progress is a thoughtful and carefully considered approach to solving the needs of the homeless in the Argus County community. The funds requested in this proposal to the Argus County Community Fund would provide the core support needed to begin implementation of one component of Partnership for Progress: The Homeless Resource Center.

Needs Statement:
The Challenge of Homelessness in Argus County

Estimates of the number of homeless individuals in Argus County vary widely, from a low of 3,000 (Argus Social Institute) to 15,000 (University of Pleasantville School of Social Welfare). But one fact is clear: as an area of particularly high poverty rates and an inadequate stock of affordable housing, Argus County accounts for a large share of the homeless population in our state. According to the 2000 census, 11.8% of Argus County's population and 17.3% of its households are below the poverty level. The County's Community Development Department noted in its 2002 study that the number of families who qualify for subsidized housing exceeds the available units by two to one. This makes Argus County one of the most poverty-stricken areas in the state and one in which homelessness is widespread.

In fact, Pleasantville, the largest city in Argus County, is one of two cities with the lowest per capita income in the entire state. Unemployment is also a significant problem in Pleasantville. Employment Development Department figures show Pleasantville's unemployment rate to be twice as high as that of the rest of the state. Ethnicity is another major factor that differentiates Argus County from the rest of the state on the issue of unemployment. A much larger percentage of the county's population is African-American than in the rest of the state—42.9% compared with 12.0% statewide. More than 50% of the state's African-American population resides in Argus County. Unemployment and homelessness have historically run much higher among this ethnic group than others.

The Pleasantville Interfaith Alliance operates the Hospitality Center, a soup kitchen for those who are homeless or at-risk of homelessness. The Hospitality Center is located in Prospect Park, one of the city's poorest areas. Most of its clients come from Prospect Park and two adjacent neighborhoods. Poverty statistics for these three neighborhoods, composed of six census tracts, are shown in the following table.

Poverty Statistics for Argus County Residents

Census Tract	2000 Population	# in Poverty	% in Poverty
3650 North Pleasantville	3,491	1,705	51
3760 Prospect Park (North)	5,035	1,806	36
3790 Prospect Park (South)	6,196	1,911	31
3770 Northside	5,291	1,461	28
3800 Northside	3,433	1,087	32
3810 Crocker/Plaza	5,750	1,495	26

The problem of homelessness in Argus County is compounded by the lack of a multiservice center for individuals and families struggling to move themselves from living on the streets to stable housing. The Needs Assessment conducted last year by United Way of Argus County placed a homeless resource center at the top of its list of priority needs. United Way notes that Lenora M. Bird, Ph.D., Director of the Department of Social Welfare at Excelsior State University and architect of the very successful Homelessness Mitigation Project in the state capital, credits the creation of a resource center for homeless families for much of the success of that Project.

Apart from stable housing, the need most frequently expressed by homeless Argus County families interviewed for the United Way's assessment is for a site where they can comfortably congregate; shower; do laundry; receive mail, information, and phone messages; access referral services; access independent living and other educational and vocational services; develop social relationships that can lead to shared housing and peer support; and generally become involved in pro-social, constructive, and therapeutic activities. The following comments from the needs assessment are typical:

"I hate it that I have to send my kids to school looking so raggedy. But I just can't afford to do laundry more than once or twice a month. And we have nowhere to take a shower." (homeless mother of three)

"I applied for three jobs that I know I'm qualified for, but I couldn't give a local address or phone number so they could reach me."(auto mechanic, single father)

The poverty of Argus County and the lack of a resource center for homeless families in Pleasantville demonstrate the need for the Homeless Resource Center planned by Partnership for Progress for the Pleasantville community.

We'll stop here because the rest of this sample proposal is identical to the one that appears previously in this chapter. Although the *meat* of the proposal describing the project to be funded remains the same, the changes in the *heart* of the proposal, establishing the need for the project, are substantial.

First of all, most of the final paragraph of the first section has been completely eliminated. Only the final sentence has been retained and now serves to "sum up" the Needs Statement and transition to Goals and Objectives. The new local statistics on poverty, unemployment, the lack of affordable housing, and estimates of homelessness in Argus County and Pleasantville are much more pertinent than the national statistic on homelessness in establishing the need for this project RIGHT HERE, RIGHT NOW. It takes only a few minutes to do an Internet search and access census data for any locality (state, city, census tract, zip code) in the United States. A search on the Web sites of groups like the local United Way or county social service agencies will often turn up studies and other data to help you document your community's need. A quote was added from a recognized (but fictitious) authority, Dr. Lenora M. Bird, who has good credentials and has run a successful program elsewhere.

You will also notice that the need for a resource center for homeless persons has been validated by local agencies and by the people to be served. Just two short quotes from prospective clients clearly illustrate the rationale for the resource center without exploiting the clients or manipulating the reader with overly emotional tone or content.

> **GRANTWRITING TIP!**
> To access demographic census data about your geographical target area, go to http://factfinder.census.gov. Other resources for data pertinent to your target area are the United Way and large local foundations who may have conducted a needs assessment.

"MAKING THE CASE" IN THE NEEDS STATEMENT

In this chapter, we demonstrated the shortcomings of a proposal that didn't "make the case," because it assumed the reader didn't need persuading. By choosing a few pertinent statistics, citing appropriate studies or other data, describing the target population, and showing evidence of local support for the proposed project, our "plain Jane" proposal was transformed into a convincing charmer.

The debate among grantmakers about using client stories and quotes may continue to rage, but the judicious selection of a few of these add color and life to your words. Just remember to balance the emotion of this subjective information with hard data.

The elements of a successful Needs Statement demonstrate to a prospective funder that you know your community and its needs. A strong Needs Statement will also provide the data a reviewer must have to present your case to the decision makers. Make sure you do your homework so the reviewer doesn't have to!

Too Much of a Good Thing

Taming the Statistician

In the preceding chapter, we wrote about the importance of establishing the need for your project. It isn't an overstatement to characterize the Needs Statement as "the heart of the proposal." You must demonstrate to the reader that the project you propose is *important* enough to merit funding, that it is *extensive* enough to warrant the amount you are requesting, and that it is *urgent* enough to be funded right now. This is what the Needs Statement must accomplish.

As we point out in Chapter Three, The Case of the Missing Needs Statement, one time-honored way to powerfully convey the importance, extent, and urgency of the problem you want to address is through well-chosen statistics. In fact, 84 percent of the grantmakers responding to our survey checked statistics as an essential element for a compelling Needs Statement.

Lori McGlinchey of the Open Society Institute says, "Statistics and data, if judiciously applied and connected to the narrative, can help the reader see how a particular proposal fits into a larger field."

Including this kind of data in your proposal also conveys to readers that you and your organization are knowledgeable about your geographical and program service areas.

But there is a fine line between validating the need and demonstrating your expertise on the one hand and putting your reader to sleep with too much data on the other. Let's take a look at the Introduction and Needs Statement of a proposal written by someone who couldn't tell the difference.

Lydia E. Girarde Memorial Clinic

Proposal to the Martia G. Santos Family Foundation
for a Collaborative Diabetes Education Program
to Serve West Polaris County

Introduction

With this proposal the Lydia E. Girarde Memorial Clinic of West
Polaris County requests a grant of $125,000 from the Martia G. Santos
Family Foundation to start a Diabetes Education Program in West
Polaris County. In our low-income, multiethnic community, the
incidence of diabetes is alarming and medical care is geographically,
economically or culturally inaccessible to many. As a result, a significant number of those with diabetes are undiagnosed and treatment
is clearly inadequate.

For these reasons, our board of directors, composed of medical professionals and local community leaders, has designated the proposed
Diabetes Education Program as its number one priority for funding
this year. Every board member has made a financial contribution
to the start-up fund with $23,000 received to date. Because of the
Santos Family Foundation's personal interest in diabetes management,
we hope that the Foundation's Trustees will want to join us in this
important work.

Needs Statement

According to the American Diabetes Association, 6.3% of the U.S.
population or 18.2 million individuals are diabetic. Appallingly, nearly
one-third of those afflicted (5.2 million) do not even know they have
the disease.

Diabetes strongly correlates with age and ethnicity occurring more frequently among older persons and amongst Blacks, Hispanics, Native Americans (American Indians and Alaskan Natives), and Asians/Pacific Islanders. For instance, 18.3% of all Americans age 60 or older are diabetic. The rate among non-Hispanic blacks is 11.4%. For Hispanic/Latino Americans it is 8.2%; for American Indians and Alaskan Natives 14.5%. Asian Americans, Native Hawaiians and other Pacific Islanders are two times more likely to have diagnosed diabetes than white residents of Hawaii of similar age. Studies also show that diabetes (Type 2) is becoming more common among Native American/American Indian, African American and Hispanic and Latino children and adolescents.

Diabetes is a serious illness with grave consequences. It can lead to a number of severe health complications such as:

- Cardiovascular—Both heart disease rates and the incidence of strokes are two to four times higher among adults with diabetes. 73% of adults with diabetes also suffer from high blood pressure.
- Blindness—12,000 to 24,000 people are afflicted with diabetic retinopathy every year.
- Kidney Disease—Those with diabetes are at high risk for end-stage renal disease; diabetes accounts for 43% of all new cases of this life-threatening condition.
- Nervous System Disease—60–70% of diabetics experience nervous system damage.
- Amputations—More than 60% of lower-extremity amputations (those not due to trauma) are performed on diabetics.
- Dental Disease—Nearly one-third of diabetics have severe periodontal disease.

- Pregnancy Complications—Poorly controlled diabetes can lead to serious birth defects and can endanger both mother and child.

The costs of diabetes are enormous. The American Diabetes Association estimates that the direct medical expense of treating diabetes was $92 billion in 2002. When indirect costs such as disability and work loss are added in, the total comes to a staggering $132 billion.

What does this mean for Polaris County, specifically for West County where our health center operates? As the tables below demonstrate, we can expect the incidence of diabetes in West Polaris County (highlighted portion of each table) to be higher than it is in the rest of the county since the population shows a larger than average number of low-income, minority and elderly individuals.

Regional Distribution in Polaris County, Population by Age

Region	>18 Years	18–44 Years	45–64 Years	65+ Years
Central	102,713	147,574	78,207	33,029
East	35,045	45,936	19,735	9,109
West	49,500	75,855	38,784	18,706
Total	187,258	269,365	136,726	60,844

Source: U.S. Census, 2000.

Percentage of Households in
Polaris County Below Poverty

Region	Total Households	% of Countywide Total	% of Households Below Poverty	% of County's Households Below Poverty
Central	9,339	53.6	9.4	39
East	2,330	13.4	16.0	17
West	5,735	33.0	17.3	44
Total	17,404	100.0	9.4	100

Source: U.S. Census, 2000.

Regional Distribution in Polaris County,
Racial and Ethnic Composition

Racial/ Ethnic Group	Number of Persons (Central)	Number of Persons (East)	Number of Persons (West)	County Total	% of Total
White	337,614	88,331	111,768	537,713	84.7
Black	4,156	8,675	47,315	60,146	9.5
Asian	13,308	4,038	14,085	31,431	5.0
American Indian	1,980	1,407	1,577	4,964	—
Total	357,058	102,448	174,745	634,251	99.2
Hispanic	19,980	18,864	18,247	56,091	8.8

Note: Hispanics are counted in all racial groups.

Source: U.S. Census, 2000.

Extrapolating from these statistics, we estimate that there are anywhere from 3,500 to more than 7,000 diabetics in West County. This is borne out in our own clinic statistics. More than 45% of our patients have a diagnosis of diabetes. Among our older clients, the rate is even higher.

Lifestyle (diet and exercise) can have a dramatic effect on the incidence and successful treatment of diabetes, especially Type 2 diabetes, the most common diagnosis (90–95% of all diagnosed cases). Unfortunately, resources to provide information on diabetes and support for lifestyle changes are scarce for low-income individuals in West County. The local chapter of the American Diabetes Association has only one outreach worker to organize public presentations and provide information for the entire county. In 2004, all outreach presentations (33) took place in Central County with most (30) held at the county hospital in Sugarland City. The driving time from West County to the hospital ranges from 25 minutes (at midnight) to over an hour at peak hours. The average is 40 minutes according to the State Department of Transportation. While public transit serves the hospital, because the trip involves making two connections, it takes 47 minutes at nonpeak hours and as much as 90 minutes at peak hours for West County residents.

Furthermore, all publicity and information for the information and outreach sessions is English-only and because of negative experiences in the past, many minority persons avoid using the county hospital. Last year we conducted a survey of our own clients. Of the 1,102 who responded, 99% prefer to receive services at our clinic. 56% have used services at other West County medical facilities. Only 2% have used services at the county hospital and 77% would elect to seek health care services in West County or not at all. Additionally, English is not the first language for 44% of our clients and 25% speak little or no English. For non-English speakers and limited English speakers, the first language breakdown is as follows: Spanish (62%), Cambodian (21%), Laotian (10%), Chinese (5%), Russian (1.5%) and Other (less than 1%).

St. Rose Hospital sponsored a diabetes information and support program in West County until July of last year when the hospital closed. Since that time there has been a 65% increase in requests from the doctors at our clinic for a local outreach, information and support program that is culturally competent to serve their patients with diabetes.

DANGER! INFORMATION OVERLOAD AHEAD

Whew! We're exhausted by that onslaught of data and statistics. How about you?

This kind of statistical overkill can be lethal. Sandra Sinclair of the J. W. McConnell Family Foundation points out, "Be careful; too much of this can make it deadly to read, without adding any value."

You certainly don't want to put a prospective grantmaker to sleep! Besides, including too much data can decrease the effectiveness of even the most compelling statistics. There are several attention-grabbing statistics in the "ugly duckling" proposal example, but their potency is diluted because there are just too many to absorb. We'd be willing to bet that if we asked you to repeat one or two statistics from the proposal you just read, you'd be hard pressed to do so without at least scanning through the proposal again.

The three sets of data shown in table format really put this proposal over the top in terms of information overload. Besides, the tables take up much more space than the useful information they contain warrants.

Furthermore, because it is difficult (maybe even impossible) to hold all that data in your consciousness at once, the writer is putting the burden on the reader to select the data to be retained. If all the reader remembers from this proposal is that Caucasians make up nearly 85 percent of the population of Polaris County, and this ethnic group is at low risk for diabetes relative to other ethnic groups, the case the writer has been trying to make is lost.

Diane Sanchez of the East Bay Community Foundation says, "If I get too much [data] I assume you don't know what data is key so you just dump everything you can find into the request."

Remember, too, that often the initial reader is not the decision maker. A program officer may have to prepare a summary of your request for the trustees who will make the funding decisions. Make their job easier by choosing only the most compelling statistics to make your case.

Although nearly every grantmaker responding to our survey mentioned the importance of statistics in establishing needs, they were also nearly unanimous in advising judicious selection of just the right statistics. "Provide only the necessary statistics and be as brief as possible," cautions Ronald D. Jones of the Siebert Lutheran Foundation, Inc.

Mario Diaz of the Wells Fargo Foundation advises, "Statistics should not overwhelm the request. They should be included to back up the local program/project need."

And Robert Walker of the Frank H. and Eva B. Buck Foundation says proposal writers should include "statistics that make the case, but not statistics just for statistics sake."

What are the "right" statistics for a proposal? Well, for starters, local statistics for local projects are best. National statistics can set the scene or provide context, but they should be backed up with local numbers. Virginia Elliott of the United Methodist Health Ministry Fund makes this point when she says, "Statistics should be relevant to the scope and goals of the program. Citing national caries rates in young children doesn't do much to support the need for a one-time toothbrush distribution in a local child care center."

The best statistics are also as current as possible and very pertinent to the program being proposed. Lina Paredes, Liberty Hill Foundation, says, "Statistics drawn from reliable sources are very strong, but they should be current, specific and geographically relevant to the problem."

GRANTWRITING TIP!
Statistics should be:
- current
- local
- pertinent
- compelling

SINGING YOUR OWN SONG: THE ROLE OF AGENCY STATISTICS

What about data from your own agency's statistics? If you're turning away more people than you are serving, isn't that a good indication that your program is needed? Yes, agree some of the grantmakers responding to our survey. Elizabeth M. Lynch, Massachusetts Bar Foundation, suggests including "not just general statistics, but also [some] from the organization. It would be helpful to know how many people they have to turn away due to limits in program capacity resulting from insufficient funding. I would encourage grantseekers to include both system-wide statistics (ensuring they are current and from a reputable source), as well as statistics drawn from their own work." And Christine Elbel of the Fleishhacker Foundation says, "Groups should also have data tracking clients served or other outcomes (tickets sold, etc.)."

THE RIGHT STUFF: HOW WILL YOU KNOW?

How will you know when you have just the right amount of just the right statistics? Well, we'd be misleading you if we said we could give you an exact formula for success. Proposal writing is still part art, part science. And there are a few funders who prefer more data than others.

Though he is hardly typical, James R. Posner of the Posner-Wallace Foundation says, "Provide moderate amount in the body of text; and lots more on a CD as appendix. Give it to us in a format where we can drill down and massage the data if we choose." His preference for detailed data in CD format is certainly unusual among the grantmakers we surveyed, but the fundamental dictum "know your funder" comes into play.

Beyond that, it may be helpful to remember the purpose of statistics in establishing needs. As we pointed out at the start of this chapter, the proposal must convince the reader that the problem you want to address is important and the needs are urgent. You also want to convey an idea of the scope of the problem. For example, how many people are affected? Or how large is the geographical area involved? For each point you want to make, try to pick the most current and compelling, even startling, statistics that accomplish this. If you feel you're overwhelming the reader with too much data, examine each statistic according to these standards: Does it grab attention? Is it specifically pertinent to the project I am proposing? Does it show the extent of the problem? Does it convey urgency?

Let's revisit the proposal from our friends at the Lydia E. Girarde Memorial Clinic of West Polaris County to see if we can create a more balanced approach.

Lydia E. Girarde Memorial Clinic

Proposal to the Martia G. Santos Family Foundation
for a Collaborative Diabetes Education Program
to Serve West Polaris County

Introduction

In our low-income, multiethnic community, the incidence of diabetes is alarming. Because medical care in West County is geographically, economically, or culturally inaccessible to many in our region, a significant number of diabetics are undiagnosed and treatment options are clearly inadequate. Education and support for prevention strategies are also unavailable in the region.

For these reasons, our board of directors, composed of medical professionals and local community leaders, has designated the Diabetes Education Program as its number-one priority for funding this year. Every board member has made a financial contribution to the start-up fund, with $23,000 received to date. Because of the Martia G. Santos Family Foundation's personal interest in diabetes management, we ask the Foundation's Trustees to consider a grant of $125,000 to start "Living with Diabetes," an outreach, prevention, and education program for clinic clients and the general public in West County.

Needs Statement

Diabetes is a serious illness with grave consequences. It can lead to a number of severe health complications, including heart disease, strokes, kidney disease, blindness, nerve damage, loss of lower extremities, gum disease, and pregnancy complications. The costs of diabetes—both direct medical costs for treatment and indirect costs such as disability and work loss—are enormous.

According to the American Diabetes Association, 18.2 million individuals in the United States are diabetic, and of these an appalling 5.2 million (nearly one-third) do not even know they have the disease. Furthermore, diabetes strongly correlates with age and ethnicity, occurring more frequently among older persons and among Blacks; Hispanics; Native Americans (American Indians and Alaskan Natives); Asians; and Pacific Islanders. Studies also show that Type 2 diabetes, which can be prevented or delayed with lifestyle changes (diet and exercise), is becoming more common among Native American and American Indian; African American; Hispanic and Latino children and adolescents.

What does this mean for Polaris County, specifically for West County where our health center operates? There are more than 18,000 persons over 65 living in West County and 44% of these households are low-income (U.S. Census, 2000). Furthermore, even though only 28% of the County's total population lives in West County, it accounts for 79% of the county's Black population, 45% of its Asian population, 33% of its Hispanic population, and 32% of its American Indian population. Because the population of West County includes a larger-than-average number of low-income, minority individuals, we can expect the incidence of diabetes and its attendant costs to be higher than average. Based on the demographics, we estimate that there are anywhere from 3,500 to more than 7,000 diabetics in West County. This is borne out in our own clinic statistics. More than 45% of our patients have a diagnosis of diabetes. Among our older clients, the rate is even higher.

Lifestyle (diet and exercise) can have a dramatic effect on the incidence and successful treatment of diabetes, especially Type 2 diabetes, the most common diagnosis (90–95% of all diagnosed cases). Unfortunately, resources to provide information on diabetes and support for lifestyle changes are scarce for low-income, ethnic-minority individuals in West County.

The local chapter of the American Diabetes Association has only one outreach worker to make public presentations and provide information for the entire county. This individual focuses outreach efforts in Central County, where the county hospital is located. Most informational sessions are held at the hospital in Sugarland City, a 40-minute drive or 70-minute transit ride for West County residents. Furthermore, all publicity and information is English-only, and because of past misunderstandings with medical staff arising from cultural differences, many minority persons avoid using the county hospital. According to a survey of our own clients conducted this year, 77% would elect to seek health care services in West County or not at all. In addition, English is not the first language for 44% of our clients, and 25% speak little or no English.

St. Rose Hospital sponsored a diabetes information and support program in West County until July of last year, when the hospital closed. Since that time, the doctors at our clinic have been clamoring for a local outreach, information-and-support program that is culturally competent to serve their patients with diabetes. With the launch of Living with Diabetes, the Lydia E. Girarde Memorial Clinic will become the only provider of multilingual and culturally competent information-and-support services to those with diabetes in West County.

MASTERING THE NUMBERS

What an improvement over the previous version! From all the data in the earlier proposal, the writer selected the right information to make the case for this project in a logical, step-by-step order. Notice that the first paragraph of the Needs Statement outlines the main points of the case: diabetes is a serious illness with grave consequences for health as well as enormous costs. The long bulleted list of serious health and medical problems caused by diabetes, which took up nearly half the page in the old proposal, has been summarized in just one sentence.

The next paragraph gives some national statistics to frame the issue and its meaning for the local community. The number of people who are unaware of their own diabetes is startling. This is a good demonstration of using a compelling statistic to good effect. "Dramatic statistics make the strongest statement," states Laurie Craft of the Grand Rapids Community Foundation. The correlation of diabetes with age and ethnicity in this paragraph will have implications for the local population, and these are made clear in the next paragraph.

After giving the local demographic statistics, the writer draws the conclusion that he or she has been leading up to: the size of the target population. It's important to interpret the data you include in your proposals, and grantmakers responding to our survey commented on this. For instance, Sandra Treacy of the Stone Foundation says, "Data alone is not helpful unless there is some analysis of it. What this data means is. . . ." And Elizabeth M. Lynch of the Massachusetts Bar Foundation adds, "It is frustrating to receive proposals that suggest there are significant needs not being met and that additional funding would solve the problem—and yet, there is no information to suggest why there is a gap, how large a gap in services exists, and how additional funding would change the ability of the organization to meet the need."

The proposal goes on to document the level of existing services for diabetics in Polaris County and the indications of the need from the organization's clinic practice for the specific type of services being proposed. From the paragraph in the ugly duckling proposal about the clinic's survey of its patients, the writer has selected only the key data. This subtly makes the point that because of the cultural competency of the clinic's staff, the target clients for the proposed Diabetes Education Project are more likely to use the services of the clinic than any other health services available in the County.

The net result of all this judicious trimming is that this part of the proposal is a full 40 percent shorter than the "ugly duckling" version we saw earlier. All that data has been distilled into a much more manageable—and memorable!—portion for the reader to digest.

There are other enhancements to the proposal as well, most notably to the Introduction. The opening sentence of the old proposal: "With this proposal, the Lydia E. Girarde Memorial Clinic of West Polaris County requests a grant" is the equivalent of starting a letter with "Enclosed please find" and not very exciting. By switching the order in this section, the proposal has a stronger opening—one that draws the reader into the emotion of the cause and entices him or her to continue reading.

SUMMING UP STATISTICS: PLAYING THE NUMBERS GAME TO YOUR ADVANTAGE

Statistics are an essential part of a proposal's Needs Statement. They establish the importance and urgency of the problem to be addressed as well as its magnitude. A startling statistic can also capture the attention of the reader and compel her to read on.

In the age of the Internet, finding data to include in proposals is relatively easy. The challenge is to select the best statistics to accomplish your goal from the proliferation of information that is available. The danger is that you will include too many statistics, and that can make for a mind-numbing proposal.

In choosing statistics for your proposals, remember that you are trying to convey *importance, size,* and *urgency.* Data from credible sources can be dramatic, relevant, and current, and, if presented in a logical order, will help you accomplish your goal.

Evaluation

Making Sure the Proposal Measures Up

I n Chapter Two, "Disorganized Proposals: Bringing Order to the Chaos," we provided an outline for the typical proposal and pointed out the logic to the sequence. Each section listed in the outline follows up on issues and themes raised in preceding sections and points logically to ensuing sections.

The Summary gives the reader a synopsis of what is to come, followed by the Organizational Background (including the agency's History and Mission), which offers more detail about the applicant and the subject area in which it works and establishes the agency's credibility. The Problem Description or Needs Statement identifies the target population and demonstrates why the proposed project is necessary. The Goals and Objectives state intended results and the Methods section describes how the applicant will go about addressing the needs and achieving the objectives. This is followed by the Evaluation section, which says how the project will be assessed, and by the Plan for Future Funding, which addresses sustainability issues.

By leading the reader through this rational progression, the proposal is trying to convey a message: "This project makes sense, and you should fund it because it will achieve results you desire." Following this line of thought, it's reasonable for funders to expect specific performance benchmarks at the outset of a grant and some demonstration of results at its conclusion. Hence the importance of Goals and Objectives and the description of Evaluation measures in a proposal.

It sounds simple enough, but we've seen far too many well-intentioned folks with excellent ideas for good community services stopped dead in their tracks during program planning when faced with setting measurable outcomes and describing how these will be measured. We've also seen proposals offer vague objectives and describe weak evaluation measures. Worst of all, we've been chagrined to discover that no data are available for a post-grant report to a funder because the evaluation measures in a proposal were an afterthought, thrown in by the writer to meet the requirements of an application.

What causes this angst about goals, objectives, and evaluation? Part of it comes from confusion about the terms themselves. How is a *goal* different from an *objective?* What are the criteria for *good objectives?* What is really meant by *evaluation?* Another part of the distress comes from performance anxiety. How do you set reasonable expectations for a brand-new program? What if the benchmarks are set too high and you fail to reach them? Will this hurt your chances with this grantmaker in the future?

Funders themselves admit to some ambivalence about their requirements for objectives and evaluations from applicants. "Generally evaluation is the most elusive aspect of the proposal," says Linda Appleton of The Health Trust. "Agencies generally don't have the resources to provide a formal evaluation, and most funders (ourselves included) do not automatically support the evaluation piece with additional funding."

Lori McGlinchey of the Open Society Institute acknowledges the limitations of evaluation with this advice to grantseekers, "Be honest about the difficulty of evaluating certain kinds of programs; the success of a program should not be evaluated solely by the number of clients served or amount of additional money raised. Change often happens slowly, and foundations and grantees should face the fact that lots of money is wasted on attempts to evaluate programs. Sometimes you really just know success when you see it."

In the face of grantmaker ambiguity and grantseeker anxiety, it is tempting to be deliberately vague about setting goals and objectives and to gloss over the measurement of results. How does it affect your chances for funding when you give in to this temptation? How important are evaluation measures to grantmakers anyway? And just how sophisticated do your tracking methods have to be to satisfy most funders? The question about the importance of evaluation is the easiest to answer. Judging from the comments we got from the grantmakers we surveyed, all of them expect at least some attempt at measuring results from their grantees.

Barbara Kemmis of the Crossroads Fund advises applicants to "demonstrate some system they have in place in their organization by which they will measure improvement and learning over the course of the grant."

Alice Cottingham of Girl's Best Friend Foundation says, "Any approach could work, as long as it is clear what the organization/program set out to learn, what they learned, and how that information was plowed back into the work to enhance or end it. I want to get the sense that the organization is committed to learning as it goes."

Sandra Treacy of the W. Clement & Jessie V. Stone Foundation adds, "I want to know what will be changed, how will foundation dollars make a difference, and how we will know the effects. I am interested in how a grantee defines success for itself, and how it captures the data, both quantitative and qualitative, to get at that. And I am interested in how they will use that analysis of the data in the future."

But what if you don't reach the targets you set out in your proposal? Does this make the project and your agency a failure in the eyes of the funder, precluding any future funding from that source? Although we didn't ask this question directly in our survey, most funders seem more concerned with the learning that should take place in such cases. Many comments, like some of those just stated, referred to the role of evaluation in helping agencies learn so that they can upgrade their performance and improve future outcomes. Grantmakers as well as others in the nonprofit sector consider evaluation a part of *best practices*. Grantmakers don't expect perfection, but they do think it's logical to seek data and feedback about the cost-effectiveness, quality, and efficacy of the programs you provide. That way, you know if what you're doing is working or if you're just spinning your wheels. Good feedback will help you improve the quality of your services and their effectiveness.

It's clear from these comments and those from other grantmakers that all funders expect some efforts at tracking grant results. The challenge to grantseekers is not whether to evaluate but how to decide what to measure and how to do it. In the typical proposal outline described at the start of this chapter, all of the sections of the proposal relate to every other part, but the Goals and Objectives section and the Evaluation section have a particular relationship distinct from that of other parts. Stated simply, the Goals and Objectives set the standards to be met and the Evaluation says how you will tell if those standards have indeed been met. Because of that special relationship, we're going to consider these two sections together even though they are not consecutive sections in the typical proposal outline. Remember that the section describing the methods usually comes between the Goals and Objectives and the Evaluation sections in a typical proposal. Keep that in mind as we consider excerpts—from three proposals this time—so that we can see samples of bad, better, and best.

We'll start with an "ugly duckling" proposal from the Lydia E. Girarde Memorial Clinic. In Chapter Four, we looked at their use of statistics in the Needs Statement for a Diabetes Education Program in the fictitious Polaris County. This time, we'll focus on two excerpts: the Goals and Objectives section and the Evaluation section.

Lydia E. Girarde Memorial Clinic

Proposal to the Martia G. Santos Family Foundation
for a Collaborative Diabetes Education Program
to Serve West Polaris County

Goals and Objectives

Our goals for this grant are to reduce the incidence of preventable diabetes and to reduce medical complications among those already diagnosed as diabetic. Our specific objective for the one-year grant period is to start a Diabetes Education Program for our clinic clients and the general public in West Polaris County.

Evaluation

At the end of the one-year grant period, we expect that the Diabetes Education Program will be up and running to serve the West County community. This will include classes, individual consultations and a resource Web site. A report on activities of the DEP and a full accounting of the expenditure of grant dollars will be provided to all funders.

OBJECTIVES THAT AREN'T

There are a couple of problems with these extracts. The stated goals, though worthy, are pretty vague and general. Are they trying to address their goals throughout the world or just in a specific community? What is their service area and who are they trying to reach? The objective, which at least mentions the target population and area, is really not an objective at all, but a statement of the method the clinic will employ to accomplish its goals. Confusing methods for objectives like this is a common problem in proposals. Objectives are the measurable outcomes of the proposed project. They need to describe what will change as a result of the methods to be employed and by how much.

> **GRANTWRITING TIP!**
> Remember that Objectives do not answer "how" the work will get done. Save the answer to that question for the Methods section.

When we teach proposal writing, we like to tell our students that objectives are always SMART. This is just a mnemonic device to help us remember the essential characteristics of objectives—that is, objectives are

- *Specific:* They are not vague or general. They make it clear what will change and for whom.
- *Measurable:* Good objectives indicate the level of change to be attained.
- *Attainable (or Achievable):* The targeted outcomes must be ones that can reasonably be expected.
- *Realistic:* In addition to being attainable, they must be reasonable in terms of cost-effectiveness.
- *Time-Specific:* They must indicate the time period allowed for their accomplishment, which is typically the grant period.

Measured against this standard, it's clear that the Goals and Objectives in the preceding proposal are inadequate. Nothing denotes the level of change that is expected. In fact, there is nothing to indicate that any change will take place at all.

This leads directly to the difficulties in the Evaluation section. Because the goals are vague, the description of evaluation techniques is also vague. Because the objective did not propose any measurable change as a target, there is no description of measurement techniques.

> **GRANTWRITING TIP!**
>
> One clue to good objectives is the presence of numbers indicating the desired degree of change. For example,
>
> - To raise reading test scores of Elm School's fifth graders by 1 grade level
> - To lower the incidence of influenza among Senior Residents by 10%
> - To increase the audience for O'Grady Players productions by 15%

MAKING A DIFFERENCE

On the positive side, the writer at least understands the necessity of providing some feedback about the results of the grant to the funder. But what kind of report can the funder expect? A grant report that says in effect, "We spent the money the way we said we would and we did the things we said we would do," doesn't answer the most important question the funder will have: "Did it make a difference?"

Let's look at the goals and objectives and the description of evaluation techniques in the second of three draft proposals for the Diabetes Education Program.

Lydia E. Girarde Memorial Clinic

Proposal to the Martia G. Santos Family Foundation
for a Collaborative Diabetes Education Program
to Serve West Polaris County

Goals and Objectives

Our goals for this grant are to reduce the incidence of preventable diabetes and to reduce medical complications among those already diagnosed as diabetic in West Polaris County. Our specific objectives for the first year are as follows:

- To hold 100 half-hour public informational sessions on the prevention, treatment, and management of diabetes at schools, hospitals, senior centers, and other public venues in West County
- To conduct 15 one-and-a-half hour classes in "Diet and Exercise in Diabetes Management" with attendance of at least 10 participants at each
- To provide one-on-one consultation to 30 diabetics on managing the disease
- To establish a "Living with Diabetes" page on our Web site

Evaluation

At the end of the one-year grant period, we will be able to demonstrate completion of the following:

- 100 informational sessions about diabetes in West County
- Attendance by 150 individuals at classes in "Diet and Exercise in Diabetes Management"

- One-on-one consultation for 30 persons on managing diabetes
- "Living with Diabetes" resources available via our Web site

Sign-in sheets at each informational session and class will provide a count of the number of sessions/classes held and the attendance. Agency records will provide a count of individual consultations. At the end of the one-year grant period, the project director will provide a narrative report on the number of project activities and people served. The report will also provide the URL of the "Living with Diabetes" page on our Web site. A full accounting of the expenditure of grant dollars will be attached to the narrative report.

PROGRESS, NOT PERFECTION

This is an improvement over the earlier draft. In this version, the goal is more specific, with the mention of the geographical target area. And at least these objectives have some numbers attached to them—a sign that something is going to be measured. The Evaluation section also does a better job by describing how performance data will be gathered.

The number and type of activities and the number of participants described in this proposal are good examples of *process objectives.* The Web page to be produced with grant funds is a *product objective,* or tangible output of the grant. The evaluation methodology is simply to count the activities and clients and show the product.

If this were a small-budget project, this kind of evaluation might satisfy some funders, as several grantmakers responding to our survey point out. "Especially for small grants, agency statistics are enough," says Jacqueline Young of the Langendorf Foundation.

Sister Janet Burkhart, HM, of the Sisters of the Humility of Mary also seems to refer to simple counting of clients when she comments, "We like to see how the results/outcomes relate to our mission; e.g., how many people who are financially poor were helped."

And Mary Gregory of Pacific Foundation Services confides, "Some [foundations] care very little [about evaluation] because their satisfaction comes in making the grant."

BEYOND BEAN COUNTING

However, many, if not most, grantmakers admit they are often looking for more than the simple "bean counting" of a process evaluation. "We want more than the numbers who walk in the door," says Ann McQueen of the Boston Foundation. Jan Eldred of the California HealthCare Foundation adds, "What we expect depends upon the specific project; there should be a way to determine whether the project has achieved the goals and objectives stated in the proposal."

"An excellent proposal demonstrates the long-term impact (both individually and in the community) that the program has achieved," states Carole M. Watson of United Way of the Bay Area. And Mary Vallier-Kaplan of the Endowment for Health states emphatically, "Outcomes evaluation is always required" by her foundation.

It helps to know the difference between a process evaluation and an outcome evaluation. In the better-but-not-yet-best proposal just quoted, methods are still masquerading as objectives. They tell us what the applicant plans to do, not why or how these activities will make a difference.

An outcome evaluation, on the other hand, answers a different set of questions. What will the measurable outcomes be for those participating in the Diabetes Education Program at the Girarde Clinic? Will participants change their diet or lifestyle as a result of the program? Will the program actually prevent at-risk clients from developing diabetes? Will it help those with diabetes manage the disease better so that they delay or lessen health complications? Answering these kinds of questions will provide information about outcomes and impacts.

How effective will outreach activities be in attracting the target population? Will those with diabetes or at risk of contracting the disease actually use the services? What do clients think about the breadth and depth of services? Will they continue to participate in program activities and will they recommend that others participate? Answering these questions will provide information about service quality, another aspect of program feedback that interests funders as does cost-effectiveness of funded projects.

Virginia Elliott of the United Methodist Health Ministry Fund sums up this approach when she advises applicants, "Describe what will be measured and how in each of four dimensions: productivity, cost-effectiveness, quality assurance and client-centered outcomes."

THE LANGUAGE OF LOGIC

In our survey, many grantmakers talk about logic models when we asked for their feedback on objectives and evaluations. It is beyond the scope of this book to provide detailed information on logic models, but so many grantmakers mentioned using or requiring them for grantees that we wanted to offer at least a simple explanation of their terminology and use. Some common terms used in many logic models are *inputs, process, outputs, outcomes,* and *impacts.*

- *Inputs* are the items required to implement a proposed approach to a problem—things like staff, equipment, site, materials.
- *Process* refers to the things you do with this stuff—that is, the project activities like tutoring sessions, art classes, performances or exhibits, or in the case of the example in this chapter, classes and consultations on diabetes and the Web site of resources for diabetics.
- *Outputs* mean the number of clients and the number of times project activities will be administered.
- *Outcomes* are the end results—that is, the changes that will lead ideally to your ultimate goal. Outcomes can be short-term ("50 clients will report positive changes in diet and lifestyle during the grant period") or long-term ("30 clients will report perseverance in positive diet and lifestyle changes in follow-up surveys two years after the grant period").
- *Impacts* measure the changes created through the outcomes. In our example, evidence of positive impacts might be a lower rate of diabetes in clinic patients or fewer serious health complications among diabetic patients at the clinic.

Using this terminology, the *process and product objectives* in the last proposal—number of services offered and people served and the Web site—are *outputs.* The stated goals—prevention of diabetes and reduction of medical complications from the disease—point to an *outcome,* but no specific outcomes or impacts are targeted in the objectives.

IT PAYS TO PLAN AHEAD

One of the reasons that so many funders pay so much attention to objectives and evaluation is because this is one way they can gauge the amount of thoughtful planning that went into designing the proposed project. Poor objectives and evaluations often reflect poor planning. "Too many organizations don't think deeply about measures," confides Ann McQueen of the Boston Foundation.

Whether your prospective grantmaker insists on a logic model or not, it's important to think through the project in an orderly way, moving from Needs to Objectives to Methods to Outcomes to Evaluation. This kind of thoughtful planning will ensure a higher success rate for your proposals. But it will also discipline you to build outcome measurement into the program at the outset. This will make it easier to prepare reports to funders and to demonstrate success to future prospects.

"One foundation I work with asks the program to frame their evaluation and figure out what techniques they will use and describe that IN THE PROPOSAL so that they don't get to the end of the grant period and find that they don't have the evaluation information they need in order to write the report," explains Mary Gregory of Pacific Foundation Services.

Other grantmakers also advise planning ahead for evaluation. For a new program, "I would encourage the applicant to get a professional evaluator to build the evaluation into the program design," says Andrea L. Reynolds of the Community Foundation of Greater Memphis.

PRACTICE MAKES PERFECT

Even though the second draft is better than the first ugly duckling in this chapter, can there be an even better job? Let's look at one more version of this proposal. This time, the proposal will include a simple outcome evaluation methodology.

Lydia E. Girarde Memorial Clinic

Proposal to the Martia G. Santos Family Foundation
for a Collaborative Diabetes Education Program
to Serve West Polaris County

Goals and Objectives

The ultimate goal of the Diabetes Education Program (DEP) is to lower the incidence of preventable diabetes in the West Polaris County community and to reduce serious medical complications among those already diagnosed as diabetic. Our expected outcomes for the first year of the program are as follows:

- At least 500 West County residents will receive basic information on diabetes through attendance at DEP informational sessions.
- At least 150 West County residents will plan lifestyle changes as a result of attendance at one of DEP's Diet and Exercise in Diabetes Management classes.
- 30 diabetics or at least 50% of those receiving one-on-one consultations with DEP counselors will report improvements in disease management.
- 50 persons per day will be accessing information on "Living with Diabetes" via our Web site.

Evaluation

The Diabetes Education Program (DEP) will be evaluated at three levels by answering the following questions:

- Did we provide the planned services? Did we reach our target population?

Attendance rosters and agency records will provide data on the number of informational sessions, classes, and individual consultations held and the attendance at each. Agency records will provide further detail (ethnicity, income level, sex, city of residence, age, diabetes predisposition factors) on the profile of those receiving individual consultations. We will also track the number of hits to the "Living with Diabetes" resources on our Web site.

- Did services produce the desired outcome?

Those attending informational sessions, classes, and individual consultations will be asked to complete a simple questionnaire to assess whether they learned new information and what lifestyle changes they plan as a result. Project counselors will hold follow-up sessions with those who participate in individual consultations to monitor whether planned lifestyle changes have been made and kept and if clients have experienced decreased risk indicators or improvements in managing their diabetes. Follow-up phone calls will be made to those not attending follow-up sessions to elicit their feedback.

- How can we improve our outreach and/or our services?

Project staff will review the list of informational sessions and classes and attendance at each of their regular quarterly meetings to determine which venues and times attract the largest number of our target population. Promotional materials and activities will also be reviewed for effectiveness. Planned adjustments in scheduling and promotion activities to maximize attendance will be noted in the minutes for each meeting.

Feedback from clients on the effectiveness of all the project activities will also be sought via the questionnaires and follow-up phone calls and through our Web site. The questionnaire will ask specifically how the program might be improved and what additional services are desired.

At the end of the grant period, the project director will gather and analyze all of the evaluation data and prepare a narrative report on the DEP and its effectiveness in meeting project goals and objectives. This report along with a full accounting of the expenditure of grant dollars will be distributed to all project staff and funders.

This proposal does a much better job of addressing objectives and evaluation. Notice that the goal specifies the target population and also points to a change in their condition. The objectives are really outcomes—that is, they describe what will change and by how much. Note also how the objectives meet the SMART criteria outlined previously. They are *specific* in spelling out the changes to be realized by the target population. They are *measurable* in that they specify numerical benchmarks, which can be measured. They seem *attainable* and *realistic* if we take into consideration the resources to be applied (the inputs, funds, staff, expertise, and so forth) that are described in the rest of the proposal in Chapter Four. Finally, the words "for the first year of the program," which precede the bulleted list, make them *time-specific*.

The section on Evaluation describes what data will be gathered and how they will be collected to demonstrate whether or not the project has met its objectives. The information in the first bullet—schedules, attendance records, and the like— will show progress in meeting the process objectives. The second bullet describes the data collection that will show fulfillment of the outcome objectives. The third bullet addresses quality improvement. Finally, the financial accounting will provide information about cost-effectiveness and efficiency.

The outcome measurements in the second bullet also demonstrate another common practice in good evaluation. Because this project is looking for long-term changes in the health of a group of individuals, practically speaking, it will be difficult to measure in the short-term. Rather than waiting, say, five years, to see if the project has had the desired effect, the clinic has devised a way to measure some intermediate outcomes or markers that point to eventual success. These are changes in the following:

- *Knowledge:* specifically knowledge about diabetes
- *Attitude:* decision to make lifestyle changes
- *Behavior:* success in maintaining lifestyle changes

PROCESS EVALUATION OR OUTCOME EVALUATION: HOW TO DECIDE

In our survey, we asked grantmakers to choose which evaluation methods and techniques they prefer when reviewing proposals. Thirty-eight percent checked "agency statistics," which are ordinarily measures of process objectives. Thirty-five percent checked "client satisfaction surveys," which usually measure service quality. Sixty-five percent marked "formal outcome evaluation systems," which shows the prevailing preference for this type of evaluation. Less than 20 percent advised using an outside evaluator.

It's important to note that many grantmakers chose more than one option and many qualified their choices with comments that said, in effect, "It depends." They pointed out that in some cases and for some funders, a simple counting of clients and services is sufficient, whereas at other times and for some funders, a more thorough outcome evaluation is required. How do you decide when each is appropriate? Based on comments from our panel of grantmakers, there are three things to consider before making this decision:

- *The preferences of the grantmaker.* "Follow the funders' requirements" is the recommendation from David Steven Rappoport of the Maine Health Access Foundation. This is always good advice! Read the guidelines and other information from grantmakers carefully and look for clues about their preference. Some may be satisfied with a process evaluation; some may require the use of a specific logic model; others may suggest an evaluation by an independent evaluator. And often funders who require more sophisticated evaluative methods will also provide funding for it or technical assistance to develop appropriate evaluation tools.

"The Foundation has often provided funding to organizations . . . to secure the services of a professional evaluator," says Cheryl Taylor of the Foellinger Foundation. Judith L. Woodruff of the Northwest Health Foundation explains, "We provide an Evaluation Workshop to teach nonprofits how to do a simple, yet complete evaluation plan using instruments that are easy to use and low cost." Molly White of Nike says that Nike also uses "custom evaluation programs conducted by a Ph.D. . . . for all NikeGO grant programs. We therefore don't ask our grantees to provide extensive evaluation, but instead to participate in the evaluation programs we already fund."

• *The size of the grant.* Even simple evaluations require staff time to gather data. More sophisticated assessment may require expertise that the agency does not have on staff. In either case, evaluation costs money. "The guiding rule for us is that the evaluation plan should fit the project. For a small program, a professional evaluator may cost more than the budget of the program. . . . [but] as a project grows, its evaluation strategy needs to evolve with it," points out Elizabeth M. Lynch of the Massachusetts Bar Foundation. Denise San Antonio Zeman explains, "Obviously, a larger more complex project will require a more complex evaluation; however, a smaller grant would be more simple."

• *The size, history, and sophistication of your organization.* As Aaron Jacobs of Social Venture Partners Seattle says, "This is not one size fits all. You have to take into consideration the size and maturity of the organization. A $10 million organization that has been around for 20 years sure better provide some outcomes from a professional evaluation. A $100,000 organization that is two years old should be able to track their outputs, maybe do some client satisfaction surveys, and should be basing their programs on research or another organization that can show positive outcomes. Then there is everything in between."

EVALUATING ARTS ORGANIZATIONS: HOW TO MEASURE A SYMPHONY

If you are writing proposals for an arts organization, you may be wondering if any of this applies to you. Indeed it is very difficult to measure the "effectiveness" of arts organizations. How do you put a value on what happens when you view a beautiful painting or attend a stimulating play? How do you measure the benefits of hearing a symphony or listening to a poem?

It's reassuring to know that those who fund the arts recognize the futility of trying to "measure" artistic endeavors. "The arts are difficult to quantify," admits Liesel Fenner of the New England Foundation for the Arts. "You can try and measure attendance, but that's difficult for artwork sited in public space. How do you measure the joy one feels from experiencing art? . . . Evaluation is very challenging to conduct in the arts, and with limited resources I usually don't promote professional evaluation." She ends with this advice: "Create art, not more reports."

But before you heave a sigh of relief and cross evaluation off your proposal outline altogether, we invite you to think about what kind of feedback arts funders may be interested in. Liesel Fenner offers these suggestions: "Stories from audiences, from both viewers and active participants, are key. We look closely at the public dialogue created by art: reviews, web blogs. Did the art project spawn other activity?" Pam LeRose of the West Virginia Humanities Council adds her own list of objectives/evaluation methods for arts organizations: "Target audience, promotional plans, audience benefits, future plans beyond the grant project."

OBJECTIVES AND EVALUATION: SUMMING UP

In this chapter, we have talked about the importance of evaluation to grantmakers. All funders want some kind of feedback on the grants they make, but the level of sophistication they require can range from a simple counting of clients served or services delivered to evaluations based on sophisticated logic models.

As you decide which evaluation technique to incorporate in your project planning, you will need to consider each funder's preferences as well as the size of the request and the maturity of your organization. This is clearly not a one-size-fits-all decision. Incorporating evaluation into program planning and doing a good job of describing measurement techniques in proposals will improve the success rate of grant applicants. It will also make the job of reporting to funders relatively pain free.

Budgets
Telling Your Story in Dollars and Cents

Cheryl Clarke refers to budgets as "translating your story from words to numbers" in the chapter on budgets in her previous book. This gives some indication of the importance of the budget in a proposal. The budget must tell the story, the whole story, and nothing but the story—and it must do it in dollars and cents. Although we could devote an entire book to the subject of budgeting for proposals, we will only devote this one chapter in order to point out some key problem areas.

Virtually every grantmaker will ask you to include a budget with your application. If your request is for program or project support, you will probably need to include *both* a program (or project) budget *and* a copy of your agency's overall annual budget. This is because funders will want to see the financial relationship of the program to the agency as a whole. On the other hand, if your proposal seeks general operating or unrestricted support, then you will only enclose your agency's overall budget.

Some grantmakers allow applicants to submit budget information in the format typically used by the agency, whereas other grantmakers insist that applicants use their prescribed format. A few funders will even provide an actual form that they want applicants to use. Given the variance in acceptable budget content and form, it is critical for you to determine, if at all possible, the specific preferences of each funder you are approaching. This information is likely to be in the guidelines or on the grantmaker's Web site. Make sure you follow the guidelines carefully.

SPOTTING FINANCIAL FLAWS

What does a typical project budget look like and what are the common problem areas in budgets? Let's take a look at a budget below that was prepared for the sample proposal from Chapter Three for the homeless resource center—Partnership for Progress—and see if we can spot the financial flaws it contains. (Note: You may want to refer to the proposal narrative that begins on page 64 as you review the budgets in the current chapter.)

Partnership for Progress:
Proposed One-Stop Homeless Resource Center

Salaries and Wages	
Program director	$ 6,500
Social workers	$ 67,500
Money management staff	$ 30,000
Employment staff	$ 20,000
Peer counselors	$ 18,762
Fringe benefits and payroll taxes	$ 22,330
Subtotal Salaries and Wages	$165,092
Other Direct Expenses	
Consultants, professional fees	$ 5,000
Building improvements	$ 18,000
Equipment	$ 40,000
Supplies	$ 18,000
Printing and copying	$ 1,800
Telephone, fax, Internet	$ 12,000
Postage and delivery	$ 1,200
Rent and utilities	$ 24,000
Miscellaneous	$ 33,880
Subtotal Other Direct Expenses	$ 120,000
Indirect Costs	$ 30,000
TOTAL EXPENSES	$ 320,000

There are several problems with this budget. Let's start with the most obvious issue first. The grand total at the bottom of the spreadsheet doesn't add up! It's pretty obvious that the math should be correct in a budget. A funder might give an applicant the benefit of the doubt and assume that a small error of a dollar or two could be the result of rounding in the formulas of a spreadsheet. But in this case, the total is off by more than $4,000! How did this happen? It could be the result of an error in one or more of the formulas in the spreadsheet. It's easy for this to happen when a budget goes through several modifications before it reaches its final form. Or perhaps the person preparing the budget started with the bottom line number of $320,000 and tried to build a budget to get to that total. In any case, when your budget is in its final format, it's always wise to sit down with a calculator and add up all the columns and rows in a budget to be sure it is computationally correct.

> **GRANTWRITING TIP!**
> Use a calculator to check the math after preparing
> your budget with a spreadsheet program.

MATCHING THE WORDS WITH THE DOLLARS

Another major cause for concern is the lack of correspondence between the budget and the proposal narrative. The proposal budget must be the mirror image of the proposal narrative in financial terms.

In this case, the staff positions named in the budget don't correspond to those mentioned in the proposal. Though it's not necessary to mention every staff position for the project in the proposal narrative, the ones that *are* mentioned should show up in the budget. The proposal specifically mentions case managers, but there are no case manager positions in the budget. Are the social workers in the budget meant to be the case managers? Maybe so, but don't leave your reader guessing.

Also, the grand total is not the same as the budget amount cited in the proposal. The proposal narrative makes reference to a "$300,000 line item operating budget for the first year of the Homeless Resource Center," but the total in the budget is $320,000—or $315,092 if you do the math correctly! Inconsistencies like this will only confuse the funder or make them doubt the applicant's ability to handle a grant.

The budget also includes a fairly large line item ($18,000) for Building Improvements, but there is no mention of this in the proposal. A budget should reflect all the expenses indicated by the narrative, but it is not the place to introduce a significant project component.

> **GRANTWRITING TIP!**
> Always do a final reading of the proposal and the budget to spot any inconsistencies between the two.

WHERE'S THE REVENUE?

But the most glaring error may be the lack of information about project revenue. Funders make it clear that when they use the term *budget*, they mean expenses *and* revenue. "I cannot tell you how many times people send only one or the other. These are meaningless by themselves since they do not offer a point of comparison," says Sandra Treacy of the Stone Foundation.

"Some think a budget does not include income," says Judith Murphy of the Y&H Soda Foundation. "We expect to have a clear picture where all funds are received and disbursed."

It's also essential to be realistic in projecting revenues. Andrea L. Reynolds of the Community Foundation of Greater Memphis mentions "unrealistic revenue projections" as one of her pet peeves in our survey. For example, if the XYZ Foundation never makes grants larger than $25,000, it's not a good idea to include a grant of $40,000 from them in your projected revenue. Or if your agency has never raised more than $50,000 from individual donors, projecting future donations of $80,000 for your project is not going to impress a grantmaker but may make them doubt your judgment.

> **GRANTWRITING TIP!**
> Don't forget to show revenue in your budget. Grant-makers want to know where your agency anticipates getting the money—and how much you realistically anticipate raising.

Other survey respondents also comment that too often applicants fail to offer many specifics about sources and amounts of revenue. Nancy Wiltsek of the Pottruck Family Foundation says, "For revenue, I want to see total amounts from individuals, government, fee for service, but foundation support should be provided in detail with name of foundation and amounts (received and pending)."

THE DEVIL IS IN THE DETAILS

In addition to the lack of information about revenue, the budget just described suffers from a lack of detail in several expense areas as well. For instance, the line item labeled Miscellaneous is $33,880—more than 10 percent of the total budget and quite a bit larger than several other line items. A funder might wonder what is included in that category. Is this where the applicant hides the executive director's slush fund? Probably not, but it's best not to leave this to the funder's imagination.

As a rule of thumb, we recommend that you consider including a narrative explanation for any individual line item that equals or exceeds 5 percent of the total budget. Line items for costs of 5 percent or less than the total budget are minimal and are not likely to grab the funder's attention.

In our survey, funders express widely different viewpoints on the amount of budget detail they want and how they want it presented. Grantmakers were about evenly split between wanting as much budget detail as possible and those seeking "moderate" or "medium" detail.

"Moderately detailed line items" are what Anne Vally of the James Irvine Foundation wants presented. "For example, line items for advertising, rent and meeting expenses are helpful. A single line item for 'staff' is not."

Jan Eldred of the California HealthCare Foundation expects "enough [information] to understand how the funds will be used."

Mario Diaz from the Wells Fargo Foundation says, "[The] budget should include dedicated staff time, materials (if necessary), program stipends (depending on the program outreach), [and] pending funding sources."

Mary Gregory of Pacific Foundation Services hopes to see "enough info in each line item for me to understand where the organization's priorities lie, but not so much that it's overwhelming."

Nancy Wiltsek of the Pottruck Family Foundation seeks a balance between wanting moderate and lots of budget detail. She says, "It depends. Ideally, I want to see revenues and expenses on one or two pages. . . . For expenses, I want to see major categories with detail only if it's relevant. For example, in the organization budget, things like postage, supplies, equipment, etc., can be collapsed into office expenses, but on a program budget, I prefer to see those line items listed."

Funders who want highly detailed budget information include Lori McGlinchey of the Open Society Institute, who says, "[I want] as much as possible, but presented clearly."

"The more the better," says Molly Talbot-Metz of the Mary Black Foundation.

Ann McQueen from the Boston Foundation comments that she wants "fairly detailed" budgets, noting, "I often have to ask for more info."

Finally, Mary Vallier-Kaplan from the Endowment for Health says she wants "lots" of information. "We ask for a budget narrative with the budget to explain the details of each line item. We also ask for committed and uncommitted revenues."

A small group of responding funders noted that they require "little" or "low" budget detail. This includes Laura Sanford of SBC Foundation, who prefers budgets that are "all broad categories, e.g., personnel, supplies, technology, etc."

> **GRANTWRITING TIP!**
> When it comes to preparing the budget, first check to see how much detail the funder wants.

BUDGET NARRATIVES

Mary Vallier-Kaplan was not alone among program officers in suggesting that grant applicants should submit a narrative along with the budget. A dozen of our survey respondents specifically mentioned budget narratives as something they expect to see when reviewing an agency's budget.

"We like to see a budget that includes all costs by line item and is accompanied by a narrative," says Elizabeth M. Lynch of the Massachusetts Bar Foundation.

A budget narrative is an explanatory note that provides the justification or rationale behind a specific line item. For example, in a $100,000 program budget with a line item of $10,000 for Equipment, it would be appropriate to include a narrative explanation as to what specific equipment will be purchased or rented and whether or not this is a one-time cost that the agency will incur or a reoccurring cost every year.

It's also the place to answer the question, "How did you get this number?" by providing the formula or the individual prices that make up a line item. For instance, the note "$10 per participant X 12 months" would be an appropriate explanation of a line item for Program Supplies.

The budget narrative is also a good place to explain the Indirect Costs line item. What are indirect costs anyway? When an organization operates more than one program, it can be difficult to divide some general agency costs among the various programs. For instance, the leadership of the executive director benefits all programs but may not be easy to classify as a direct program expense. Likewise, insurance, the audit, fundraising, and accounting expenses and some office expenses may be difficult to allocate among the programs but are necessary to the effective functioning of the entire organization. These costs can be covered by including a line item for Indirect Costs in each program's budget. This is usually figured as a percentage of the direct costs, and a budget narrative would be the place to list the percentage being used.

> **GRANTWRITING TIP!**
> A budget narrative is the place to explain specific line items and the rationale behind the costs.

THE FINANCIAL MAKEOVER

By paying careful attention to detail and by providing the potential funder with accurate, well-presented information, your budget will be clear and you'll increase the chances of success (see budget on next page).

Good budgets reflect good planning. This revised budget will go a long way toward reassuring a grantmaker that proper planning has been done. In addition to making sure all the columns and rows add up so the math is computationally correct, several other changes were made to transform the "ugly duckling" budget into a "beautiful swan." The revenue sources are clearly identified at the top of the budget. In addition, by dividing the budget into columns, the way expenses will be allocated among the funding sources is clarified. The status of each revenue source

Partnership for Progress:
Proposed One-Stop Homeless Resource Center: Revised Budget

REVENUE SOURCES	Notes	County Block Grant	County Social Services Department	Ella Hogans Community Services	Pleasantville Interfaith Alliance	Grants	TOTAL
Status: P = Projected, S = Application Submitted, A = Approved		$125,000 A	$22,500 A	$15,000 A	$18,762 P	$134,000 $78,000 S $56,000 P	$315,262
EXPENSES							
Salaries and Wages							
Program director	1 FTE	$6,500				$6,500	$6,500
Case managers	1.5 FTE; includes .5 FTE as in-kind contribution from County Social Services	$45,000	$22,500				$67,500
Money management staff	1 FTE					$30,000	$30,000
Employment staff	1 FTE					$20,000	$20,000
Peer counselors	Pleasantville Interfaith Alliance volunteers; in-kind contribution calculated at $18.04 per hour as per Independent Sector valuation of volunteer time				$18,762		$18,762
Fringe benefits and payroll taxes	@ 22%	$11,330				$11,000	$22,330
Subtotal Salaries and Wages		*$62,830*	*$22,500*	*$ —*	*$ 18,762*	*$61,000*	*$165,092*
Other Direct Expenses Consultants, professional fees	Program share of fundraising consultant/ grantwriter					$5,000	$5,000

Building improvements	Laundry, bath facilities; accessibility	$18,000				$18,000
Equipment	Includes washers, dryers, and computers for staff and client use; includes $5,000 in-kind from Ella Hogans for office furniture and staff computers	$32,806	$5,000		$2,194	$40,000
Supplies	Laundry and hygiene supplies @ $100/month; office supplies @ $50/month; child care supplies @ $750/month; other program supplies @ $500/month; janitorial/maintenance supplies @ $100/month				$18,000	$18,000
Printing and copying	@ $150/month				$1,800	$1,800
Telephone, fax, Internet	@ $1,000/month				$12,000	$12,000
Postage and delivery	@ $100/month				$1,200	$1,200
Rent and utilities	Includes $10,000 in-kind contribution from Ella Hogans		$10,000		$14,000	$24,000
Miscellaneous	Janitorial/maintenance contract ($12,480), security contract ($20,000), IT support contract ($1,400)				$33,880	$33,880
Subtotal Other Direct Expenses		*$50,806*	*$15,000*	*$ —*	*$83,074*	*$120,000*
Indirect Costs	@ 10% for audit, payroll services, bookkeeping, insurance, general agency expenses	*$11,364*		*$ —*	*$15,000*	*$30,000*
TOTAL EXPENSES		$125,000	$22,500	$18,762	$144,074	**$315,092**

is also specified, and more detail about other grant sources is included at the bottom of the budget.

The addition of a Notes column gives details for each line item. The Full Time Equivalent (FTE) for each staff position is identified, and in-kind contributions are clearly labeled. The rationale for determining the value of volunteer hours is given. Formulas and itemized lists are given for many line items, and an explanation of the Building Improvements and Miscellaneous line items is added. This information is equivalent to a budget narrative and can be presented as a column in the budget as we have done it here or as footnotes at the end of the budget.

Several changes were made to make sure the budget matches the proposal narrative. Social Workers was changed to Case Managers to match the terminology used in the proposal. Assuming that the correct total project cost is now reflected in the revised budget, the proposal narrative will need to be revised to reflect the new number.

A new sentence will also be added to the proposal to explain the line item for Building Improvements. The addition of laundry and shower facilities and renovations to make the building handicapped accessible were not mentioned in the proposal narrative and could be deleted from the operating budget. But since the building improvements are covered by the block grant from the county—which *was* mentioned in the proposal and will cover other expenses in the budget— we have included them in the revised budget.

TO BALANCE OR NOT TO BALANCE

You may notice that the "new and improved" budget is not balanced. The total revenue is $315,262 and the expenses total $315,092. That is because most grants are made in round numbers. The block grant for $125,000, the request to the Roberta Gonzalez Foundation for $50,000, and the one to the Argus County Links for $8,000 are typical. The in-kind contribution of volunteer hours from the Pleasantville Interfaith Alliance is based on twenty hours a week at $18.04 per hour, which makes the budget come out to $315,262 instead of a nice round $315,000 or $316,000.

The expense side of a budget, on the other hand, often contains many more precise calculations—for staffing, fringe benefits, and the like—that will almost always make the budget come out to an odd number, like the amount of $315,092 in this budget. Because the projected expenses represent the applicant's best estimate of costs, funders expect that the actual amounts will come out at least a few dollars above or below the budgeted amount and most will not be troubled by a budget like this one that does not balance. But if the funder's guidelines indicate otherwise, you should make sure the revenue and expenses are balanced. One way to do that in this budget is to make this a request for a grant of $49,840 from the Roberta Gonzalez Foundation instead of $50,000.

OTHER BUDGET WOES

When it comes to budget content and presentation, program officers had much to say about what gets under their skin. In addition to the problems highlighted in our sample budget, what else drives them crazy when it comes to reviewing the numbers?

"Columns that don't line up on the page look sloppy," says Christine Elbel of the Fleishhacker Foundation. "And financial reports for completed prior years that show income and expenses as matched to the dollar look suspicious."

"When the budget hasn't been thought through. Large organizations who use boilerplate budgets and narrative and don't tailor it to the particular grant application. We see through these folks right away and it doesn't reflect well," says Liesel Fenner from the New England Foundation for the Arts.

MAKING SURE IT ALL ADDS UP

In this chapter, we demonstrated the most common and serious flaws in proposal budgets:

- Computational errors—that is, the numbers don't add up
- Missing information about revenue sources
- Inconsistency between the proposal narrative and the budget
- Failure to provide formulas, rationales, or other details for specific line items

By checking the math after completing the budget spreadsheet and by adding a revenue section and a budget narrative or notes, you can reassure a prospective grantmaker that your program planning is both thoughtful and prudent. A final careful reading of the proposal and the budget will reveal any inconsistencies between the two that should be corrected.

Remember that the budget is the way you tell your story in numbers. Make sure the numbers match the words you used in the proposal and try to anticipate questions that prospective grantmakers might ask. Answering these questions in advance will shorten your path to raising grant dollars.

Proposal Length

The Long and Short of It

In the grantseeker's version of Goldilocks and the Three Bears, proposals can be classified as "too verbose," "too sparse," or "just right." Our goal, when writing a proposal, is to say all that we need to say to most effectively present our case and no more. Yet there is often the temptation to include more than we really need to, that somehow a longer proposal seems worthier of the funding. Not so. The merits of a proposal are judged not by their weight or thickness, but by their content. The strongest proposals are those that demonstrate the effectiveness of an agency's plan of action. James R. Posner of the Posner-Wallace Foundation finds it troublesome "whenever too much or too little weakens the story."

This chapter examines the topics of wordiness and length. Like Goldilocks, you'll get to examine three versions of the same proposal and see if you don't agree that only one works best.

TOO VERBOSE

Grantmakers may have already found a solution to the problem of the verbose proposal, for many funders have adopted page limits. Page limits are rules, not guidelines. As rules, they are to be strictly observed. Program officers have been known to reject requests solely because they exceed the stated page length. Fail to adhere to this simple rule, and you'll take your proposal out of the running before the competition for funding even starts. Better to give your agency a fair shot at securing the grant by staying within the stated maximum number of pages.

The reality is that proposals can stay within the allotted page length and still suffer from acute verbosity. We shudder to think about the length of some of the submissions to funders that do not specify a page limit.

We observe, as do several of our survey respondents, that grantwriters frequently get too detailed and too verbose when writing about the methods their agency plans to use in the delivery of client services. Grantwriters, particularly novice ones, will often gloss over a full explanation of the need or problem to be addressed and then get bogged down in the Methods section of a proposal. We believe the reason for this is that grantwriters assume the reader already understands the problem or need as well as they do. But it's more often the case that the agency's specific methods are not familiar to the funder, yet they are thoroughly known by the writer. Therefore, methods get described in excruciating detail. If a writer goes overboard in her description of methods, a program officer can become annoyed.

When we asked grantmakers about annoying writing styles, Anne Vally of the James Irvine Foundation says, "Too much detail about operational matters (what youth will eat for lunch during the program break, or how much the van rental will cost for transportation), and not enough about the strategic thinking behind the program (how and why this particular intervention will make a difference for youth and what research validates the program design)."

To illustrate the problem, let's look at a sample Methods section in a proposal for the fictitious Fellowship House.

Fellowship House

Proposal to The Robert Bissinger Charitable Fund

Methods

In keeping with national trends in the field of supportive transitional housing, Fellowship House will provide its residents with a wide-range of comprehensive support services. These include: career counseling; life skills training; workshops on budgeting and financial planning; parenting and health care workshops; appropriate transportation to/from educational classes, job interviews and other career-building activities; childcare and other social services.

1. *Career Counseling.* During their stay at Fellowship House, residents will gain the skills, confidence and self-esteem needed to obtain and keep employment. Upon admittance to Fellowship House, each adult resident will be given a battery of assessment tests by a staff career counselor to determine his/her level of academic achievement, English language fluency, personality traits, and career interests/aptitudes. It is anticipated that about half of the incoming residents will have graduated from high school, while the other half will have not. It is also anticipated that none of the incoming residents will have taken any college-level courses. It is further anticipated that for 25% of the incoming residents English will not be their primary language.

Once the results of the assessment tests have been reviewed and analyzed by the career counselor, he/she will meet with the new resident to discuss the findings. These meetings will be scheduled for one hour during the business day and will take place in one of the small conference rooms located in the administrative office area at Fellowship

House. Given the importance of helping resident clients find appropriate employment, several career-exploration meetings may be needed and will be scheduled with the resident. At these meetings, the career counselor will present the resident with various appropriate career options. The resident will have ample opportunity to discuss his/her goals, aspirations and interests, as well as to ask questions of the career counselor and gather information. The career counselor will discuss each potential employment field and what skills and educational background are necessary to gain entry-level employment in the various fields. Written materials prepared by local employers, trade associations, and community colleges, as well as supplemental information prepared by Fellowship House staff, will be made available to the resident.

An individualized career path plan will be designed for each resident. Depending on each individual resident's chosen career interest, the plan may require the resident to obtain additional schooling or training. If so, the career counselor will work with the resident to find the most appropriate school or preparatory program, taking into consideration such factors as cost, transportation, and admissions criteria. Fellowship House staff have already made connections with Stony Point Community College, a local community college, and nearby trade schools.

In addition to one-on-one career counseling sessions, Fellowship House will also host a variety of optional career-related workshops that will be open to all residents. Topics will include: interviewing skills and workplace etiquette, how to write a resume, grooming and dressing tips, and negotiating employment terms. Workshops will be organized by Fellowship House staff. Presenters will include Fellowship Hall staff and members of the local community who have expertise in a given area. Outside presenters may include career counselors from Stony Point Community College, professional employment coaches and representatives from regional employers. These group workshops are intended to augment the individual one-on-one meetings and to reinforce information presented in other forums.

Since the majority of residents will be busy taking classes during the day, generally career-related workshops will be offered in the evenings and on weekends. They will be held in the main floor conference room at Fellowship House and will last between one and two hours. Given the evening hour, light refreshments and beverages (water, coffee and tea) will be served. While it is hoped that light meals, such as sandwiches and salads, will be donated by local grocery stores, the program budget includes this line item should Fellowship House be unable to secure these donations. Supervised childcare for children ages 12 and under will be provided so parents will not have to miss these important group workshops. Children will be able to read, draw, play board games and watch videos. Healthy snacks and refreshments will also be provided.

The goal of the career counseling aspect of the program is to provide each adult resident at Fellowship House with a "game plan" for choosing a career field and then taking the necessary steps to find entry-level work in their chosen area. Securing and obtaining employment is critical for formerly homeless individuals to make the successful transition from poverty and homelessness to financial stability and permanent shelter.

2. *Life Skills Training.* A companion program to the career-counseling component of supportive services is the life skills training. In the

optional life skills training workshops, Fellowship House staff will teach all residents essential skills such as learning how to read a public transit schedule, balancing a checkbook and comparative price shopping.

The majority of the residents in Fellowship House will have spent a considerable amount of their adult life homeless and living on the streets before finding stabilization through an intermediary transitional housing program that prepares them for this more intensive transitional living situation. Because most residents will have spent a significant portion of their lives on the street—some since their teen years or younger—they will not have learned essential living skills that they will need in order to succeed independently.

The life skills sessions are designed to be interactive and very hands on. Residents will be challenged to identify appropriate bus and subway routes to various locations in the Metropolitan City area. Field trips are also planned to a neighborhood ATM and grocery store. At the ATM, staff will demonstrate how to make a deposit and how to withdraw cash. At the grocery store, residents will have an opportunity to "buy" items from a pre-prepared grocery list, and thereby learn how to select among the different brands by evaluating nutritional content and by making price comparisons based on weight and volume of the food item. Life skills classes will be presented twice monthly in the early evening. Each class will last about 1½ hours and childcare will be provided, along with light refreshments that will be similar to those served at the group career counseling workshops.

WAY TOO MUCH DETAIL

We stop the proposal at this point. This fictitious Methods section continues with a detailed description of the workshops on budgeting and financial planning; parenting and health care workshops; transportation to and from education classes and various job-seeking activities; child care and other social services.

Whew! There's a lot of information in the previous Methods section, most of it extraneous and certainly more than most program officers would need—or want. So far, the writer has covered two of five major support services provided to the residents of Fellowship House. The writer presumably could continue with similarly detailed descriptions of the other support services: workshops on budgeting and financial planning, parenting and health care workshops, transportation to and from educational classes, job interviews and other career-building activities, child care, and anything else. But enough!

When printed on an 8½-by-11 sheet of paper with standard one-inch margins, this Methods section excerpt already fills nearly two pages. If we consider the two most likely scenarios, the problems with this example are glaring.

In the first scenario, we'll assume that the prospective grantmaker has stipulated no page limit so the proposal can be as long as the writer sees fit. Even without a page limit, the proposal is way too long. The writer has included too many irrelevant details about operational matters rather than program strategy.

Consider this sentence from the third paragraph: "These meetings will be scheduled for one hour during the business day and will take place in one of the small conference rooms located in the administrative office area at Fellowship House."

It is doubtful that any program officer will be interested in either the length of the career counseling meetings or where they will be held. The grantwriter could better use the space to discuss the importance of one-on-one career counseling as an effective strategy in assisting the formerly homeless to secure employment.

There are numerous other examples of extraneous details in this proposal, from the planned refreshments at evening meetings to a list of the activities children may participate in while in child care. This information doesn't contribute to the presentation of a persuasive case for support. Rather, it bogs the reader down in pointless minutia. Before we get bogged down ourselves, let's consider a second likely scenario.

The second scenario contemplates a proposal for Fellowship House that must be no longer than five pages. A five-page limit for a proposal narrative, exclusive of attachments, is fairly typical. When only five pages are available, a grantwriter can't earmark two or more for the Methods alone. There won't be enough room for all of the other components that constitute a complete proposal—namely, Summary, History and Mission, Need or Problem Statement, Goals and Objectives, Evaluation, and Future Funding. In this scenario, the grantwriter has allocated too much space to discuss the Methods at the expense of the other proposal sections.

GRANTWRITING TIP!

A balanced proposal is one where the respective sections are neither too long nor too short for the overall page length. For example, when working with a hypothetical five-page narrative limit, use the following guidelines for how much space to allocate to each section of the proposal.

- Summary—half page (10 percent of the total)
- History/Mission—one to three paragraphs (5 to 10 percent)
- Need or Problem Statement—one page (20 percent)
- Goals and Objectives—half to one page (10 to 20 percent)
- Methods—half to one page (10 to 20 percent)
- Evaluation—half page (10 percent)
- Future Funding—one to three paragraphs (5 to 10 percent)

POSITIVE COMMENTS

Though the "ugly duckling" excerpt is too long, there are a couple of positives. First, the fact that there is so much detail tells us that the grantwriter really understands the operations of the program. This is wonderful. It indicates that the writer has spent time either observing the program firsthand or talking with the program director. The writer's apparent depth of knowledge will be useful should the grantwriter have a follow-up conversation with the program officer either via telephone or during a site visit.

The second positive is found in the opening sentence, which reads, "In keeping with national trends . . ." This informs the program officer of the agency's rationale for the chosen methods. Fellowship House is not piloting a new program, it is *following* national trends. We think the writer could have said a little more about how these services have been successful, but at least he or she has touched on the justification for the agency choosing these particular services.

TOO SPARSE

On the opposite end of the spectrum is the proposal that is too sparse. This is rare. It is highly unusual for a grantwriter not to have something substantial to say about the nonprofit agency and its work. More likely, one or two sections of an otherwise fully developed proposal will get short shrift. There are many reasons why this may happen. The proposal writer may not have enough information to write about, or the writer may not think the section as important as the others, or the writer may cut corners when pressed for time.

For simplicity sake, we've continued to use the Fellowship House Methods section to illustrate when a proposal section is too sparse (see next page).

Although we advocate brevity in writing, this excerpt takes our mantra "keep it short" to an extreme! Instead of drowning the reader with irrelevant details, the writer provides hardly any information at all. In any length proposal, this Methods section is simply too short and lacks essential information. Perhaps it may suffice as a short answer to a question in a grant application form where space and word count is limited, but it is hardly a narrative description. As noted earlier, grantwriting this sparse is very rare.

JUST RIGHT

If one example is "too long" and the other "too short," can we do some remodeling and construct one that is "just right?" A good version of the "right length, right amount of detail" Methods section appears on page 123.

Fellowship House

Proposal to The Robert Bissinger Charitable Fund

Methods

In keeping with national trends in the field of supportive transitional housing, Fellowship House will provide its residents with a wide range of comprehensive support services. These include career counseling; life skills training; workshops on budgeting and financial planning; parenting and health care workshops; transportation to and from educational classes; job interviews and other career-building activities; child care and other social services.

Fellowship House

Proposal to The Robert Bissinger Charitable Trust

Methods

In keeping with national trends in the field of supportive transitional housing, Fellowship House will provide its residents with comprehensive wraparound services. These services include career counseling; life skills training; workshops on budgeting and financial planning; parenting, nutrition, health care, and wellness workshops; transportation to and from educational classes; job interviews and other career-building activities; child care and other social services. Studies show that formerly homeless individuals have a better chance of successfully transitioning to lives with stable employment and permanent housing when agencies provide them with these "bundled" services. *(National Coalition for Homeless Families 2004 Report on the Positive Outcomes of Wraparound Supportive Services in Long-Term Transitional Housing.)*

Upon admittance to Fellowship House, each adult resident will be given a battery of assessment tests to determine his or her level of academic achievement, English language fluency, personality traits, and career interests and aptitudes. It is projected that only half of the incoming residents will have graduated from high school, and for about 25 percent English will not be their primary language.

A staff career counselor will review the resident's assessment tests and then meet with the resident to discuss the findings, potential careers, and the resident's interests and aspirations. An individualized career plan, which may include further education and skills training, will be designed for each resident.

Fellowship House will also offer residents a variety of optional workshops, including ones on career-related topics, life skills, budgeting and financial planning, parenting, and health care. Speakers will include agency staff, as well as professionals and experts in their field from the surrounding community, as Fellowship House has developed strong relationships with the local business, education, and health care communities. For example, career-related workshops may feature career counselors from Stony Point Community College, professional development coaches, and representatives from area employers. The career workshops are designed to complement the individual career counseling sessions and will feature topics that are more appropriate to learning in a group setting. Among the subjects to be covered are interviewing skills, business etiquette, resume writing, and negotiating employment terms.

Because the majority of Fellowship House residents will have spent a significant portion of their adult lives living on the streets, they will not have learned the essential living skills that are necessary for successful independent living. Life skills training will be practical and hands on, providing residents an opportunity to learn essential skills, such as how to read a public transit schedule, how to balance a checkbook, and how to do comparative shopping. Workshops on budgeting and financial planning will teach residents how to budget household expenses and how to make sound financial decisions, as well as the importance of savings. To encourage healthy lifestyles and stable families, workshops will also be offered on various parenting and health issues, such as diet and nutrition, conflict resolution and discipline, and stress-relieving techniques.

Workshops will be open to all residents and held during the evenings and on weekends so as not to conflict with daytime education classes and job-seeking activities. To encourage attendance, child care and refreshments will be provided.

Transportation will be provided or arranged so residents can attend education classes, job interviews, and other employment-related appointments. Fellowship House owns a 16-passenger van that can be used to transport residents, and public transit service is conveniently located within two blocks of the residential community.

TOO LONG–TOO SHORT PROPOSAL MAKEOVER BECOMES JUST RIGHT

The first excerpt is too long. The second is too short. But the third is "just right." In this final version of Methods, the irrelevant details have been eliminated, such as what refreshments will be served and what rooms meetings will be held in. But additional relevant information has been added, such as a summary of all of the supportive services offered to residents at Fellowship House—namely, information about the budgeting and financial planning, health and parenting workshops, and transportation services.

If we return to our hypothetical five-page narrative, this mid-sized version of the Methods section fits neatly on one 8½-by-11 page—well within an acceptable range in relation to the other components of a proposal.

Another improvement concerns the rationale for the chosen methods. The first version made a passing attempt to do this by noting that Fellowship House was "keeping with national trends." The "just right" version goes one step further and cites studies indicating that formerly homeless individuals are likely to be more successful in transitioning from homelessness to stable employment and permanent housing when provided with comprehensive supportive services. The inclusion of this one sentence is significant. It provides the justification for *all* of these services. It also lets the grantmaker know that the agency is keeping up-to-date on best practices in the field.

WRAPPING UP: THE LONG AND SHORT OF IT

When asked to comment on what annoys her in proposals, Judith Murphy of the Y&H Soda Foundation says, "Detail that is not relevant."

What grantmakers want to know and need to know is usually the same thing. They want relevant information about the nonprofit agency, the clients being served, the need for intervention, and how the agency plans to intervene. Padding your story does not improve it. But don't trim so much that the reader is left with nothing but bare bones! As with many things, moderation is the key.

Split Personality

What Happens When There's More Than One Writer

Every professional proposal writer who has been in the business for more than a few months has a story to tell about a "monster" proposal. Usually, it goes something like this:

The client—a staff person at a well-respected nonprofit—calls and asks for help putting together a proposal to meet an impending deadline. "This one should be easy. I'm sure it won't take you any time at all. We have all the pieces. We just need someone to cut and paste them together and make sure we're following the funder's application instructions."

Sometimes different staff people at the agency have prepared the various pieces. Maybe the development staff did some research and wrote the Needs Statement, the program director wrote the Project Description, and the Organizational Background is boilerplate from previous proposals. The finance department contributed the Budget. Sometimes the project is a collaboration between two or more agencies, and a staff person from each agency prepared one or more sections.

In any case, many hours, dozens of phone calls to the various writers, and quite a few gray hairs later, the proposal writer finally delivers the "easy" proposal to the client for submission to the funder.

As professional grantwriters, we refer to these as "Frankenstein" proposals, ones that have been stitched together by two or more writers and they're real "monsters" because making all the parts mesh and flow into a coherent whole can gobble up enormous amounts of time and creative energy.

Can funders tell if they've received a "proposal by committee"? Most of those who answered our survey said they do notice when more than one writer has been involved. For starters, every writer has a unique style—a distinct voice—some more distinctive than others. A sudden change in style, tone, and point of view can be jarring to the reader. But this stylistic quirk rarely affects the grantmaker's decision, according to nearly every funder who responded to our survey. They either don't notice, or as Donna Gassie of the Virginia Tobacco Settlement Foundation says, "I can tell, but it doesn't influence my decision-making." There were even a few who insisted that they preferred reading different points of view—when the bookkeeper prepares the financial information and the program staff writes the project description, for instance. Or as Judith Woodruff of the Northwest Health Foundation said, "Sometimes in a collaborative proposal, I expect that to occur."

BEWARE REDUNDANCY AND INCONSISTENCY IN PROPOSALS BY COMMITTEE

However, most survey respondents qualified their answers by noting the shortcomings that can result from "proposals by committee." Mary Vallier-Kaplan of the Endowment for Health in New Hampshire points out that having multiple writers prepare an application "might influence the quality of the proposal and therefore our decision-making."

What are the problems that are likely to spell trouble for proposals with multiple writers? Redundancy and inconsistency are the most frequent flaws according to the grantmakers we surveyed. Another danger is the risk that your project may appear disorganized to grantmakers. Anne Vally of the James Irvine Foundation comments, "Yes, I can tell if more than one writer has been involved, because the proposal may seem fragmented." She goes on to say, "It's . . . unusual to see a well-organized proposal come from multiple authors."

The following proposal—a collaboration among three nonprofits—demonstrates the defects that our panel of grantmakers described—and a few others besides!

Senior Dental Access in Blue Moon County

Proposal to the Charles W. La Due Family Fund for a
Dental Health Promotion for Seniors in Blue Moon County

The Challenge of Dental Health Among the Elderly

The connection between dental health and general health is well-established. A lack of attention to dental hygiene and access to regular professional dental care leads to cavities, gum disease, pain and tooth loss. This can seriously compromise a person's ability to eat a balanced diet which has grave implications to general health. For instance, elderly persons with tooth and gum problems often limit their intake to soft or pureed foods which can exacerbate problems with regularity in digestion/elimination and also frequently leads to malnutrition.

Dental misalignments, missing teeth and ill-fitting dentures can cause sores to develop in the mouth. In extreme cases, untreated oral infections have led to serious illness and even death. For homebound seniors or those confined to long term care facilities, access to regular dental care is a challenge. Most facilities or home care services have medical personnel—nurses, doctors and podiatrists—who make regular visits to facilities serving the elderly. Unfortunately, because of the nature of dental care with its specialized equipment, even basic dental services are usually not included in these medical services.

Recent advances in technology have led to the development of hand-held dental drills and portable dental trays and other equipment. This makes it feasible to provide dental services in nursing homes, at senior centers and even in private homes. But the costs for these units are high. One complete portable, dental set-up is $15,000 and a set-up for a dental hygienist is $5,000.

Blue Moon County has a sizable population of elderly persons because Oak Grove, a large retirement community with 7,800 residents, is located here. Oak Grove serves as a "feeder community" for several large long-term care facilities located nearby. Additionally three adult day care programs, a home health service and several senior centers also operate in Blue Moon County.

Sedgwick Elder Care Services operates the two largest adult day programs in the County as well as a home care service for homebound seniors. They estimate that 60% of their 1,100 clients have compromised dental health because they are unable to access professional dental services. Blue Moon Senior Care Alliance operates three long-term care facilities with a total population of 622. Despite ongoing efforts to recruit dentists to serve their clients, it has been seven years since they have had a dentist on staff.

A recent survey of the senior centers, senior meal sites and informal, faith-based programs for seniors in the County revealed that all of them report seniors who are in critical need of dental care. Some of the meal sites report that as many as 42% of those they serve require special diets because of dental problems.

At the same time, the County boasts one of the best dental schools in the country—the University of Mars School of Dentistry (UMSD). Every year, UMSD trains 250 students in dental hygiene and general dentistry and an additional 75 in orthodontics and oral surgery. As part of their training, students must complete a substantial number of hours of clinical work. About half of the students are able to complete their clinical requirements in the three clinics UMSD operates in the communities of Venus, Uranus and Saturn. Other students must seek clinical assignments outside the County and some travel as far as the far end of Mercury County to complete their hours under the direction of licensed practitioners at clinics there. Students and professors are well aware of the dental needs of the local elderly population but have not had the necessary equipment or organizational structure to make it feasible to offer care to homebound elderly. Furthermore, the students' clinical work often does not include elderly patients so they graduate with little experience in treating dental issues in the elderly and little inclination to pursue a career in geriatric dentistry.

Objectives

During its first year, the Dental Health Promotion Project for Seniors will accomplish the following:

- Provide basic dental services to 100 elderly residents of Blue Moon County.
- Provide opportunities for clinical experience for 25 dental students and 25 dental hygiene students.
- Students will gain experience in a setting that represents a new market for viable dental practice.

Expected outcomes are:

- Dental health will improve for 100 seniors.
- Three to five students will decide to pursue a dental practice in geriatric dentistry at the completion of their coursework.

Program Planning and Funds Raised to Date

For the past year, faculty from the School of Dentistry have been meeting with staff from Sedgwick Elder Care Services and Blue Moon Senior Care Alliance to develop a plan to address the dental health needs of seniors in Blue Moon County. Working together they developed a plan and submitted a proposal to the U.S. Department of

Health and Human Services for funding. HHS has awarded a one-year $125,000 grant to launch a one-year Senior Dental Health Promotion Project as a pilot project. The HHS grant will cover the costs of one professor (a licensed dentist) to supervise the work of 30 dental students, stipends for the students, and administrative overhead.

The challenge now is to raise the funds needed for equipment—$125,000—and the salary of an Outreach Coordinator/Scheduler—$40,000. This proposal is a request to the Charles W. La Due Family Fund for a grant of $125,000 to match the HHS grant. Grant funds will be used for the Outreach Coordinator/Scheduler's salary and benefits and toward the cost of equipment.

Project Description

Three highly regarded community institutions are collaborating to provide in-home dental care to homebound seniors living in Blue Moon County, a community with a large senior population. These three agencies are: the University of Mars School of Dentistry, Sedgwick Elder Care Services, and Blue Moon Senior Care Alliance. Each institution has a long and illustrious history of providing quality service to the residents of Blue Moon. The University of Mars School of Dentistry (UMSD) was established in 1955 and we have graduated some of the top dentists and orthodontists in the state. Currently, we train 300 students for careers in dentistry and as dental hygienists, plus we have an additional 75 post-doctoral students. Sedgwick Elder Care Services ("Sedgwick"), founded in 1973, is the county's largest provider of adult day care and in-home care, presently serving 1,100 clients. The third partner in the collaboration is Blue Moon Senior Care Alliance (the "Alliance"). The Alliance is affiliated with Galaxy

Senior Alliance Centers, a national operator of residential senior communities. We operate several long-term senior care facilities in the county that serve 622 residents.

There is an undisputed connection between a person's physical health and dental health. Poor dental health, especially among the elderly, may be evidenced by symptoms such as sensitive gums, toothaches and mouth pain due to improperly fitting dentures. People with mouth or teeth pain may be unable or unwilling to eat, resulting in poor nutrition and diet. A survey of residents living in Alliance long-term care facilities revealed that the majority of our residents were on special diets because they wore dentures or had other dental issues. Alliance nutritionists prescribe nutrition-rich shakes and other liquids for some residents. Poor nutrition and diet can cause a myriad of health problems such as weight loss, fatigue, greater susceptibility to disease and infection, and the inability to ward off common ailments like colds and the flu. Fortunately, routine dental care can help prevent such health problems and enable seniors to live better lives.

What brought UMSD, Sedgwick and the Alliance together was the shared recognition that dental health is an overlooked need in the county's care of its senior citizens. While several community agencies provide homebound seniors with nursing and medical care, no organization in Blue Moon County currently offers in-home dental care. This collaboration will fill the gap by providing regular dental check-ups and care to seniors who are unable to travel to a dentist's office. Provided funding is in place, the program will begin in September at the start of UMSD's academic year.

The program will be launched in two phases. In the first six-month start-up phase, the program will target seniors living in long-term care facilities, specifically those operated by the Alliance. Commencing in the second six-month period, the program will expand to serve seniors living independently but who are unable to visit the dentist. (An estimated 60% of Sedgwick's 1,100 clients need dental care.)

Our third- and fourth-year dental students, under the supervision of their clinical professors, will provide the actual dental care. Each visiting dental team will be outfitted with portable bedside trays, hand operated drills and other essential equipment. Teams will be able to conduct routine check-ups, provide teeth cleaning, fill cavities and perform other minor procedures. Patients with serious dental problems will be referred to appropriate specialists, such as oral surgeons and periodontists.

As part of the project, Sedgwick will hire a full-time Outreach Coordinator/Scheduler who will be responsible for publicizing the program to attract patients, coordinating dental visits with the Alliance, Sedgwick and other programs and for scheduling dental appointments. We do not anticipate any problems with finding enough patients during start-up as Alliance has a sufficient pool of likely candidates. During Phase One, the Outreach Coordinator/ Scheduler will organize "Dental Clinic Days" at Alliance facilities and will conduct intensive outreach to staff and clients at Sedgwick's adult day centers and its homecare program as well as to other senior programs in the community. Outreach will consist of printed materials, mailings and in-person presentations to staff and clients at prospective host organizations. By the conclusion of Phase One, we expect that these programs will start to provide additional patients for the program for Phase Two. We expect to serve 60 patients in Phase One; an additional 50 patients will receive services in Phase Two.

Total program costs for the first year are $395,000 which includes personnel and administrative costs of $145,000 (the supervising professor's salary, the Outreach Coordinator/Scheduler's salary and administrative support) and equipment and supplies costs of $250,000. (These include 15 portable dental set-ups at $15,000 each, three portable X-ray units at $5,000 each, and miscellaneous equipment and supplies at $10,000.) Grant funds will be used toward the total needed for dental equipment and supplies. We have submitted requests to the Foundation of the Blue Moon County Dental Association and to the Procter & Gamble Fund for grants for equipment and supplies, and we also plan to use our industry connections by approaching equipment manufacturers to see if we can secure some equipment donations for the project.

Conclusion

Using UMSD dental students is beneficial. First, the program benefits because it is more economical to run because of the free labor provided by our students. Second, our students benefit because they are able to get valuable hands-on clinical experience. Third, homebound seniors in Blue Moon County benefit because they will receive quality routine dental care in the convenience of their own homes. Finally, the entire community benefits when its citizens are healthy.

LOOK WHO'S TALKING!

The writing styles aren't too discordant here, but it's pretty clear that at least two different people wrote this proposal. If you're guessing that the change in authors occurs at the Project Description, you're right. The biggest clue is the repetition. Notice how the three collaborating partners are described under The Challenge of Dental Health Among the Elderly and again in the Project Description? The second paragraph of the Project Description also restates the need and really belongs in the previous section. Repetition is a common flaw when more than one writer is involved, as Sandra Treacy of the W. Clement and Jessie V. Stone Foundation observes. "If there is more than one writer, the problem is usually with redundancy."

Another clue is the confusion in point of view. Notice the inconsistency in the use of "we," "our," and "they" for the collaborators? Although this is a minor discrepancy, it adds to the disjointed tenor of the proposal.

INCONSISTENCY: A DEADLY SIN

Redundancy and changes in voice or point of view may be annoying, but the most fatal trap in "proposals by committee" is inconsistency in the facts about the project. This "sin" can be deadly if it leads prospective grantmakers to question the ability of the applicants to coordinate their efforts effectively when they embark on the project.

Let's look at the inconsistencies in this proposal:

- Will the grant funds be used for equipment only or for staff salary and equipment? At the end of Program Planning and Funds Raised to Date, we read, "Grant funds will be used for the Outreach Coordinator/Scheduler's salary and benefits and toward the cost of equipment." But a sentence at the end of the Project Description says, "Grant Funds will be used toward the total needed for dental equipment and supplies."

- Will the students be paid "stipends" for their work or not? Stipends are mentioned toward the end of Program Planning and Funds Raised to Date but not in the final paragraph of the Project Description.

- Is UMSD's annual student enrollment 250 as stated under The Challenge of Dental Health Among the Elderly? Or is it 300 as stated in the Project Description?

- The Objectives say 100 elderly will be served, but the last sentence in the second to last paragraph in the Project Description says 60 in the first phase and 50 more in the second phase. How many elderly will be served?

- What is the total for equipment costs? In Program Planning and Funds Raised to Date, equipment is listed at $125,000, but in the itemized list in Project Description, equipment and supplies add up to $250,000.

> **GRANTWRITING TIP!**
>
> Do a careful final reading of the proposal and the budget, keeping a close watch for inconsistencies—especially when more than one writer has been involved!

STAYING ORGANIZED IN A COLLABORATION

Together these flaws make the proposal come off as disjointed and the project as disorganized. In a large-scale collaboration like this, it is absolutely essential that all partners be on the same page. Otherwise prospective funders will worry about how smoothly the program will run when it is funded.

Virginia Elliott of the United Methodist Health Ministry Fund says multiple writers might have an adverse affect on her decision "if it appears that no one has a good grasp of the big picture of the program." And inconsistencies in the facts of the project like those we've just pointed out are the most serious flaw in "proposals by committee." Several grantmakers comment on this in our survey. While acknowledging that she can tell when two or more writers have worked on an application, Andrea L. Reynolds of the Community Foundation of Greater Memphis adds, "It only influences my decision-making if the voices disagree."

Returning to the sample proposal, some key pieces are missing. For example, there is no explanation of how the collaboration will be organized. Many grantmakers encourage applicants to collaborate with other agencies on proposals, but they expect the framework of the collaboration to be crystal clear. In this example, which is the lead agency? How will oversight be handled? What are the reporting relationships between the three participating agencies?

There is also no section on evaluation. The first outcome ("dental health will improve") seems pretty vague. How will outcomes be measured? Specifically, how will improvements in dental health for the elderly patients be measured? It's always wise to plan evaluation strategies and who will implement them as you plan your program, but this is particularly important in a collaboration.

Finally, none of the partners working on the proposal bothered to make the connection to the funder's interests.

Now take a look at the revised proposal.

Senior Dental Access in Blue Moon County

Proposal to the Charles W. La Due Family Fund for a Dental Health Promotion for Seniors in Blue Moon County

The connection between dental health and general health is well-established. Access to routine dental care promotes good oral health. But for homebound seniors or those living in long-term care facilities, getting to the dentist can be at best logistically difficult and at worst impossible.

To address this challenge in Blue Moon County, three highly regarded community institutions are collaborating to provide in-home dental care to homebound and institutionalized seniors. Each of the three agencies—the University of Mars School of Dentistry (UMSD), Sedgwick Elder Care Services (Sedgwick), and Blue Moon Senior Care Alliance (the Alliance)—has a long and illustrious history of providing quality service to the residents of Blue Moon. This proposal requests funds from the Charles W. La Due Family Fund's "Healthy Aging Initiative" for the Senior Dental Access Project.

The Challenge of Dental Health Among the Elderly

A lack of attention to dental hygiene and access to regular professional dental care leads to cavities, gum disease, pain, and tooth loss. This can seriously compromise a person's ability to eat a balanced diet, which has grave implications to general health. For instance, elderly persons with tooth and gum problems often limit their intake to soft or pureed foods, which can exacerbate problems with regularity in digestion and elimination and also frequently leads to malnutrition. Poor nutrition can cause a myriad of health problems, such as weight loss, fatigue, greater susceptibility to disease and infection, and the inability to ward off common ailments, like colds and the flu.

Dental misalignments, missing teeth, and ill-fitting dentures can also cause sores to develop in the mouth. In extreme cases, untreated oral infections have led to serious illness and even death. Fortunately, routine dental care can help prevent such health problems and enable seniors to live better lives.

But for homebound seniors or those confined to long-term care facilities, access to regular dental care is a challenge. Most facilities or home care services have medical personnel—nurses, doctors, and podiatrists—who make regular visits to facilities serving the elderly. Unfortunately, because of the nature of dental care, with its dependence on specialized equipment, even basic dental services are usually not included in these medical services. In 2000, the U.S. Surgeon General noted that "nursing homes and other long-term care institutions have limited capacity to deliver needed oral health services to their residents, most of whom are at increased risk for oral diseases" [*Oral Health in America: A Report of the Surgeon General*].

In 2003, in testimony before the U.S. Senate about oral health among the elderly, Dr. Greg Folse used slides to demonstrate oral problems among nursing home residents that he said were "often ignored" and sometimes life-threatening. "It's a sin," he said. "We have to do something at a national level to ensure access to care for the low-income aged, blind and disabled" [American Dental Association press release, September 25, 2003].

Dental Care for the Elderly in Blue Moon County

Blue Moon County has a sizable population of elderly persons, because Oak Grove, a large planned retirement community with 7,800 residents, lies within its boundaries. Oak Grove serves as a "feeder community" for several long-term care facilities located nearby. In addition, three adult day care programs, a home health service, and several senior centers also operate in Blue Moon County.

Sedgwick Elder Care Services, founded in 1973, runs the two biggest adult day programs as well as a home care service for homebound seniors. They estimate that 60% of their 1,100 clients have compromised dental health because they are unable to access professional dental services.

Blue Moon Senior Care Alliance, which is affiliated with Galaxy Senior Alliance Centers, a national senior residential facilities and services company, owns three long-term care facilities in the County with a total population of 622. Despite ongoing efforts to recruit dentists to serve their clients, it has been seven years since they have had a dentist on staff at their skilled nursing facility.

A survey conducted last year of residents living in Alliance long-term care facilities revealed that the majority of seniors are on special diets because they wore dentures or had other dental problems. Alliance nutritionists prescribe nutrition-rich shakes and other liquids for about 25% of their residents because of oral health issues. A more recent survey of the senior centers, senior meal sites, and informal, faith-based programs for seniors in the County revealed that all of them report seniors who are in critical need of professional dental attention. Some of the meal sites report that as many as 42% of those they serve require special diets because of dental problems. Although several community agencies provide homebound seniors with nursing and medical care, no organization in Blue Moon County currently offers in-home dental care.

The Blue Moon County Department of Public Health has estimated that $1.5 million was spent last year to treat complications arising from seniors' lack of access to regular dental care. Beyond the dollars, the cost in human terms can be heartbreaking. The Blue Moon United Way's Needs Assessment for 2005 tells the stories of three individuals in local nursing homes. One suffered unnecessary tooth loss, one had to be hospitalized for several weeks because of a massive infection, and one endured months of pain—all because of untreated dental problems. United Way cites access to dental care as one of the top three priorities for the County's elderly.

Lack of access to good dental care in Blue Moon County is ironic because it boasts one of the best dental schools in the country— the University of Mars School of Dentistry (UMSD). UMSD was established in 1955 and has graduated some of the top dentists and orthodontists in the state. Every year, the School trains 300 students in dental hygiene and general dentistry and an additional 75 in orthodontics and oral surgery. As part of their training, students must complete a substantial number of hours of clinical work—14 hours per week for third-year students and 30 hours per week for fourth-year students. About half of the students are able to complete these requirements in the three clinics operated by the School in the communities of Venus, Uranus, and Saturn. Other students must seek clinical assignments outside the County, and some travel as far as the far end of Mercury County to complete their hours under the direction of licensed practitioners at clinics there. Furthermore, the students' clinical work often does not include elderly patients, so they graduate with little experience in treating dental problems in the elderly. This means they are unlikely to pursue a career in geriatric dentistry, further exacerbating the supply-and-demand imbalance.

Students and professors have been acutely aware of the dental needs of the local elderly population for some time but have not had the necessary equipment or organizational structure to make it feasible to offer care. Handheld dental drills, portable dental trays, portable X-ray units, and other equipment make it possible to provide dental services in nursing homes, at senior centers, and even in private homes. But the cost for these units is high. For instance, one complete portable dental set-up is $15,000.

Objectives

During its first year, the Dental Health Promotion Project for Elders will accomplish the following:

- Provide basic dental services to 100 elderly residents of Blue Moon County.
- Provide opportunities for clinical experience for 25 dental students and 15 dental hygiene students.
- Students will gain experience in a setting that represents a new market for viable dental practice.

Expected outcomes are:

Improved dental health: 100 seniors will show improvements in their dental health assessments within three months of first receiving services.

Increased practitioners: Three to five students will decide to pursue a dental practice in geriatric dentistry at the completion of their course work.

Program Planning and Funds Raised to Date

For the past year, faculty from the School of Dentistry have been meeting with staff from Sedgwick Elder Care Services and Blue Moon Senior Care Alliance to develop a plan to address the dental health needs of seniors in Blue Moon County. Working together, they developed a plan and submitted a proposal to the U.S. Department of Health and Human Services (HHS) for funding. HHS has awarded a $125,000 grant to launch a one-year pilot of Blue Moon Senior Dental Access. The HHS grant will cover the costs of one professor (a licensed dentist) to supervise the work of 30 dental students, stipends for the students, and administrative overhead. The local dental community has been very supportive of the project, and local dentists have committed to donations of dental supplies for the project. (See letter of support from the Blue Moon Dental Society in the attachments.)

The challenge now is to raise the funds needed for equipment ($225,000) and for the salary of an Outreach Coordinator/Scheduler ($45,000). This proposal is a request toward those funds.

Project Description

UMSD will serve as the lead agency and as the fiscal agent for this project. A Memo of Understanding, signed by the CEOs and Board Chairs of each of the collaborative partners, is included in the attachments. This document spells out the reporting relationships of project staff and how liaison between the three participating agencies will be handled.

The program will be launched in two phases. Provided funding is in place, the program will begin in September at the start of UMSD academic year in 2007. In the first six-month start-up phase, the program will target seniors living in long-term care facilities, specifically those operated by the Alliance. The project will provide services to 60 elderly individuals in this period. Commencing in the second six-month period, the program will expand to serve seniors living independently but who are unable to visit the dentist. Senior Dental Access will serve an additional 40 individuals during this period.

Third-year and fourth-year UMSD dental students, under the supervision of a clinical professor, who will act as project director for this grant, will provide the actual dental care. Students will be organized in 15 dental teams of one student dentist and one student hygienist. Each visiting team will be outfitted with portable bedside trays, hand operated drills, and other essential equipment. Teams will be able to conduct routine check-ups, provide teeth cleaning, fill cavities, and perform other minor procedures. Seniors with serious dental problems will be referred to appropriate specialists, such as oral surgeons and periodontists.

Sedgwick will hire a full-time Outreach Coordinator/Scheduler, who will be responsible for publicizing the program to attract patients, coordinating dental visits with the Alliance, Sedgwick, and other programs, scheduling dental appointments, collecting evaluation data, and preparing regular reports. We do not anticipate any problems with finding enough patients during start-up as Alliance has a sufficient pool of likely candidates. During Phase One, the Outreach Coordinator/Scheduler will organize "Dental Clinic Days" at Alliance facilities and will conduct intensive outreach to staff and clients at Sedgwick's adult day centers and its home care program as well as to other senior programs in the community. Outreach will consist of printed materials, mailings, and in-person presentations to staff and clients at prospective host organizations. By the conclusion of Phase One, we expect that these programs will start to provide additional patients for the program for Phase Two.

Total program costs for the first year are $395,000, which includes personnel and administrative costs of $125,000 (the supervising professor's salary at 20% FTE, the Outreach Coordinator/Scheduler's salary, stipends for dental students, and administrative support covered by the

HHS grant) and equipment and supplies costs of $250,000. Equipment costs include 15 portable dental set-ups at $15,000 each, three portable x-ray units at $5,000 each, and miscellaneous equipment and supplies at $10,000. Grant funds from the La Due Family Fund will be used for the salary of the Outreach Coordinator/Scheduler ($45,000 including taxes and benefits). The balance of grant funds will be used toward the total needed for dental equipment. The Blue Moon Dental Society is providing the supplies as an in-kind donation from its members. Board Members from all three partners in the collaboration have pledged $71,000 toward the project in individual gifts. We have submitted requests to the Foundation of the Blue Moon Dental Society and to the Procter & Gamble Fund for additional grants for equipment and supplies. Faculty at UMSD as well as the UMSD Alumni Association have agreed to approach equipment manufacturers to secure some equipment donations.

Evaluation

Data Collection

The Outreach Coordinator/Scheduler will be responsible for compiling statistics on the number of patients served, the number and type of services provided, and the number of potential clients reached through outreach activities. At the conclusion of each individual patient visit, student dentists and hygienists will complete a dental health assessment for the patient using a classification system as follows:

1. Good—Dental health is satisfactory; only regular follow-up required.
2. Stable—Some existing dental health problems, which can be addressed in next two to three visits.

3. Acute—Multiple and/or serious dental problems requiring immediate attention.

Students will forward assessments to the Outreach Coordinator/ Scheduler for entry into the project database. Patient satisfaction surveys will also be mailed to patients and participating facilities/ community organizations quarterly.

Data Reporting

At the conclusion of each quarter, the Outreach Coordinator/ Scheduler will produce a statistical report on services provided, the number of clients who have experienced improvements in their dental health assessments, and the results of client satisfaction surveys. At the conclusion of each year, the clinical professor who serves as project director will prepare an in-depth report based on statistical data and patient and participant feedback. This report will be forwarded to all funding sources and will also be used in budgeting and program planning for future years.

Conclusion

The multiple benefits that will result from this project are closely aligned with the "Dental Health: Prevention and Access" objectives of the Charles W. La Due Family Fund's Healthy Aging Initiative. Using UMSD dental students is economical because of the free labor provided by the students. Second, the students benefit because they are able to get valuable hands-on clinical experience without traveling far outside the county. Third, this experience will validate geriatric dentistry as a viable career option for participating students. Fourth, homebound seniors in Blue Moon County benefit because they will receive quality routine dental care in the convenience of their own homes. Finally, the entire community benefits when health care costs are controlled and citizens are healthy.

TAMING THE MONSTER

This rewrite accomplishes several things:

- By reorganizing and combining the repetitive elements, the redundancy is eliminated.
- A more consistent point of view ("we," "they") throughout makes it cleaner and clearer.
- The new version adds important information by naming the lead agency and describing the collaborative structure in a little more detail. An attached Memorandum of Understanding will spell it out still more. (A sample MOU is included in Resource A.)
- Adding statistics and quoting authorities strengthen the Needs Statement. A quick Internet search uncovered the two documents that are quoted as well as the evidence from local agencies. Additional data comes from client statistics of two of the collaborating partners.
- The proposal makes a much stronger case by slightly modifying the outcomes and adding an evaluation section.
- The addition of information about support from the local dental community and from board members of the three collaborators also strengthens the case as do the figures on the costs to the community because of seniors' lack of access to care.
- By naming the funder's Healthy Aging Initiative in the opening and repeating this at the end, the proposal makes the connection to the funder.

CONSISTENCY IS CRUCIAL!

But the most important change of all is making sure all parts of the narrative agree. It's never a good idea to leave doubts or unanswered questions in the mind of the reader. Make absolutely sure that facts are consistent.

All of the questions we raised about inconsistencies in the original proposal have been answered.

- We know that the grant funds requested will be used for both the Outreach Coordinator/Scheduler's salary and for equipment.

- It's clear that stipends for dental students are included in the budget.

- The student enrollment at UMSD totals 375—300 in dental hygiene and general dentistry and another 75 in orthodontics and oral surgery.

- The number of elderly persons to be served is the same in the Objectives as in the Project Description.

- The total amount for equipment is clarified.

MAKING THE PARTS ADD UP TO A COHERENT WHOLE

In this chapter, we have seen the potentially disastrous results of "proposals by committee." As Elizabeth M. Lynch of the Massachusetts Bar Foundation remarks, "It is easy to tell when more than one writer has worked on a proposal. It does not influence the final decision. What does influence the decision is if the two or more writers' components do not blend together into a coherent project proposal."

Here the job of the proposal writer is more like that of an editor. His or her role is not just to "cut and paste" but to receive input from appropriate parties and create one fluid whole out of the parts. The proposal can then be sent to those who contributed information and data with a request that they review for accuracy. Suggestions for editorial changes can be considered, but the process will go much more quickly—and the end product will be far superior—if one person exercises editorial control.

Redundancy, inconsistency, and a lack of organization are the most common pitfalls of proposals with multiple writers. Be sure to reexamine your proposals for these flaws before submitting them to grantmakers for review.

Florid Writing
When Proposals Go Over the Top

For the record, we like adjectives and adverbs. We admire a well-crafted descriptive phrase. We advocate the use of active verbs. Used sparingly, adjectives, adverbs, descriptive phrases, and active verbs can breathe creative life into your writing. Overused, they become noticeable distractions, words the reader trips, rather than glides, over.

Grantwriters are frequently told that their proposal must stand out from the others in the so-called slush pile on the program officer's desk. They're advised to write with passion, "punch it up," make it sizzle. Occasionally, writers will take this advice too far. Their writing takes on an unmistakable flair. Flowery language springs up like delicate, beautiful little daisies on the previously starkly vacant page. You get the idea. By drenching your prose with too many adjectives and adverbs, your proposal succeeds in standing out—but for the wrong reason.

FLORID, NOT FATAL

In our survey, we asked funders this question: "Are there any writing styles that are particularly annoying?" Respondents could select one or more of the following choices on our questionnaire: florid writing (too many adjectives and adverbs); academic, abstract, vague, pontificating language; too much detail; too little detail; poor grammar and spelling; and other, which gave funders a write-in option. Nearly two-thirds of the respondents checked "florid writing," indicating that they find this writing style annoying. Molly White of Nike noted that she finds florid writing "very annoying."

Annoying is a far cry from *fatal*. It is highly unlikely that a proposal will be turned down simply because it is riddled with adjectives. Yet why take the chance? Why risk annoying the person you're asking for money? As a grantwriter, your job is to educate, inform, and persuade program officers—not irritate them.

Laurie Craft of the Grand Rapids Community Foundation offers the following observation: "A good proposal is one where I have no questions about the project when I've finished reading it and I've managed to stay awake because it is not full of unnecessary words."

Florid writing and the inclusion of unnecessary words can also be detrimental when space is an issue, as it so often is. More often than not, grantmakers restrict the number of pages for letters of inquiry and proposals. It can be a challenge to squeeze everything we want to say within the confines of the page restrictions we're given. This means every word must count. You don't have the luxury to include unnecessary words and phrases. Your writing must be lean.

Cheryl Taylor of the Foellinger Foundation notes this: "Summaries are restricted to one page. It is critical for applicants not to waste their space with florid writing or pontificating language."

What does florid writing mean? If some adjectives and adverbs are OK, how many does it take before you have too many? The answer is subjective. We can't possibly quantify the number of permissible adjectives with respect to other words per page in a proposal! However, we know, and program officers know, when a writer has crossed that imprecise line and sprinkled too many descriptive words throughout a proposal.

The problem becomes fairly obvious with an example. Here's a version of a florid proposal.

Community Art and Literacy Museum
Proposal to the Noel Norton Foundation for
Tactile Textiles: A Sensory Experience **Exhibit**

CALM's Dynamic History and Captivating Mission

The Community Art and Literacy Museum (CALM) is a unique and innovative cultural oasis that celebrates the bounteous fine art and literary creations of gifted and talented local artisans who at one time or another have called Tranquil County their home. CALM's utterly captivating and inspirational mission is "to celebrate the extraordinary bounty of visual and literary arts created by Tranquil County artists so citizens of this remarkable community can be inspired, enlightened, and awakened by and to the beauty that surrounds them."

CALM was founded in 1990 by a feverishly passionate group of arts patrons, including the incomparable Poindexter Moneybags, who recognized that a dynamic artistic community was flourishing in their midst. This nucleus group also realized that the community lacked a permanent venue in which to showcase the undeniably outstanding work of local artists. One of the group's fabulous founders, Poindexter Moneybags, offered to donate his sizable collection of contemporary Tranquil County art to CALM, provided a suitable site was found and purchased and dedicated in perpetuity to faithful service as a fine arts and literary museum. For two generations, the Moneybags family has judiciously collected pieces created by the county's luminous masters, steadily building a collection that has few rivals in the contemporary art world. But it was a collection that few eyes could see for much of it resided in storage or within the sheltered walls of the Moneybags estate. However, an exceptionally enlightened Poindexter Moneybags desired to share his family's collection with the discerning general public—and CALM was born.

After the group successfully raised more than $2M from other generous families and individuals during an exciting and exceptionally challenging three-year period, CALM purchased a run-down and dilapidated 10,000 square-foot building on Taupe Town's Main Street. Following an agonizing year of major renovations, during which time the beautiful Beaux Arts building was lovingly restored to its original splendor and magnificence, the new museum was unveiled to its patrons and the general public at an exquisite gala celebration.

Today, CALM houses a permanent collection of more than 600 magnificent paintings (oil, acrylic and watercolor), sculptures, ceramics and multi-media works from Tranquil County artists, thereby showcasing the amazing talent of our local artists. In addition, CALM also presents very special exhibitions that celebrate the spirit of art generally, and new and emerging artists in particular. Yet CALM is much, much more than a county art museum for the organization is also the vibrant hub of local literary activity as it offers an ongoing series of poetry and short story readings and houses the offices of the internationally renowned literary magazine, *Simple Words*.

Throughout history, Tranquil County has been like a magnet, a beacon for artists of all disciplines, and especially those who toil with visual medium—be it paint on a canvas, clay on the potter's wheel or penned words on a page. Artists exhausted by the hustle and bustle of Metropolitan City and other urban environs have long flocked to our county's charming hamlets and villages, finding tranquility and peaceful venues within which to create. Renowned regional artists include the late Mike L. Angelo, Pablo P. Casio, and Vincent Van Go. Many of the finest works ever created by these artists hang in CALM's spacious, naturally lit galleries. Without CALM, residents of Tranquil County would have to travel more than 100 grueling miles to over-crowded Metropolitan City, where parking is scare and expensive, to view art of this caliber. We are thrilled to report that last year's attendance topped 100,000!

CALM is well governed by a 15-member board of directors that is comprised of a representative sampling of the diverse local population, including arts patrons, businesspersons, lawyers, one accountant, an advertising executive and a marketing consultant. A full one-third of our board members are people of color and eight are women—and all are fabulous. It is important to note that our board is fully committed to the proposed project.

Pinkie Starr is CALM's intelligent and resourceful Executive Director and she has performed marvelously since her hiring in 1992. Ms. Starr has a notable background in arts administration, having previously held senior administrative positions at the Louvre, the Metropolitan Museum of Modern Art and the Getty Museum. CALM has a current staff of 14 highly talented and loyal full-time employees and six equally talented and loyal part-time employees. Our superlative staff is supported in their amazing efforts by scores of dedicated volunteers who work as docents, assist in the administrative offices and provide extra helping hands for special events.

CALM's annual operating budget is $2.1M with admission fees accounting for about half of the total revenue. Other income comes from very generous grants and individual gifts (25%), unrelated business income from our outstanding cafeteria and well-regarded bookstore (15%), rental fees from lavishly hosted corporate parties, weddings and special events (9%), and interest earned on CALM's modest endowment (1%).

The Overwhelming and Crying Need for a Textile Exhibit

As noted above, CALM houses some of the finest works of Tranquil County artists. Our collection features paintings, sculptures, ceramic pieces and works of mixed media that represent a variety of styles, from realism to the abstract. While CALM's magnificent collection is among the most impressive of its kind in this fair state, regrettably CALM does not have any textile works in its permanent collection. Many visitors to the museum specifically mentioned this fact on the satisfaction surveys that are distributed to departing visitors by our dedicated corps of loyal and industrious docents. Last year, more than 50% of survey respondents indicated that they would "very much" like for CALM to either acquire textiles for its permanent collection or host a textile exhibition.

To address this most unfortunate and ghastly situation, CALM's outstanding and highly regarded Executive Director, Pinkie Starr, and inventive Head Curator, Jack Pollockson, began considering the various options regarding how to bring textiles to the museum more than five long and laborious years ago. Their painstaking exploration led them all across the country and eventually back to Tranquil County where they discovered the Tranquil County Textile Artisans Association (TCTAA), a collective of weavers and other artists who create exquisite fabrics, garments, carpets, quilts and other cloth items for retail sale and as objects d'art. Following several months of involved, complicated and occasionally tedious negotiations, TCTAA and CALM have agreed to a joint exhibition at CALM of more than 100 textile expressions in December 2007.

Given the popular appeal of textiles among the local populace, as well as the millions of visitors to Tranquil County, CALM anticipates drawing a substantial increase in museum visitors during the four-month blockbuster show, including tens of thousands of out-of-town-ers who will schedule visits to our humble county just to experience the show. Conservative estimates based on actual attendance at other blockbuster shows nationwide indicate that CALM should expect a 150% increase in museum attendance during the 120-day exhibition. As noted above, more than 100,000 flocked through CALM's doors last year or approximately 8,333 through the turnstiles each month (though actually, attendance is higher during the chilly winter months when people have fewer outdoor alternatives); therefore, we expect to see an increase to nearly 12,500 per month. This much-anticipated increase in attendance, especially from local residents who are more apt to become regular visitors, is a wonderfully glorious collateral benefit of mounting such a show. CALM plans to encourage new and repeat visitors to join our embryonic membership program, thereby bringing new sources of revenue to the fabled institution.

Therefore, for all of these excellent reasons and many, many more, it is imperative that CALM host this very, very special exhibition, which will showcase a stunning and breath-taking display of the most imaginative and aesthetically arresting textiles ever created in Tranquil County. CALM is now seeking financial support from munificent foundations and generous corporations to mount such an exceptional exhibition that will be titled *Tactile Textiles: A Sensory Experience.* As a reader can plainly see, CALM carefully crafted a frugal, yet functional, budget of $425,000 for the exhibition, which anticipates raising nearly $350,000 from foundation and corporate sponsors. Appended to our grant application are an extensive list of donor levels and the well-conceived benefits that accrue to each respective level. We dearly hope that the Noel Norton Foundation will consider a grant of $50,000 to this once-in-a-lifetime opportunity.

Problem Number One—Whatever the Count, This Is Too Many!

Are you annoyed by the lavish language in this proposal? Imagine if this is one of the 250-plus proposals you have to read. Now imagine a program officer's anguish if every one of them mimicked the style in our example.

We didn't count the number of descriptive words in this proposal, but whatever it is, it's way too many. It seems as if every noun is accompanied by a descriptive word—or more often two. Art is "bounteous." Artists are "luminous." The administration is "intelligent and resourceful." The staff is "superlative." Docents are "industrious." Art patrons are "feverishly passionate." Is anyone, or anything, ordinary in Tranquil County?

The problem with packing too many adjectives, adverbs, and descriptive phrases in a proposal is that they begin to lose their impact, particularly when they are all so impossibly affirmative. When everything is described as "great," "terrific," and "wonderful," the reader begins to wonder whether anything is actually great, terrific, and wonderful. So much hyperbole can cast doubts on the credibility of the applicant agency. A program officer can reasonably wonder whether the picture is as rosy as it is portrayed, for in the real world, nonprofits face their share of organizational challenges, obstacles, and difficulties.

Our example uses positive descriptive words in the extreme, but the same can be done with negative language. In grant proposals, problems can be described as "wrenching," "dire," "calamitous," "disastrous," and plain "horrific." Two reactions are possible. First, when the writer paints too bleak a picture, the program officer may not see even a glimmer of hope. And hopeless causes do not get funded, because grantmakers do not want to throw money down a black hole. Second, when a situation is presented as unremittingly negative, a program officer may doubt the seriousness of the claims. If everything is described as "awful," perhaps it really isn't? Once again, a shadow of doubt can fall on the credibility of the applicant agency.

> **GRANTWRITING TIP!**
> The challenge for a grantwriter is to use a light touch when sprinkling out those descriptive words—and to balance the good with the bad.

Problem Number Two—Unique and Innovative Aren't

There's a second problem with this ugly duckling proposal—and it's sitting right there in the first sentence. It's the use of the term *unique and innovative* to describe the applicant agency, which in this example is the Community Art and Literacy Museum. This overused phrase has become devoid of real meaning. Does any non-profit agency think they are *not* unique and innovative?

The reality is that some nonprofit organizations truly provide *unique and innovative* work. Others deliver *important, critically needed,* yet not *unique and innovative,* services. Saying your work is unique and innovative does not make it so. Joan McCammon of the J. W. McConnell Family Foundation dislikes it "when they [applicants] claim to be unique but they are not."

It is preferable to let the description of your agency's work tell its own story, rather than using empty phrases such as *unique and innovative.* If the work is unique, it will be obvious to the program officer. But services don't have to be unique to merit funding. Services that are needed and important, though not unique, are just as likely to be funded—provided you've presented a strong and persuasive case.

GRANTWRITING TIP!
Avoid relying on empty phrases to make your case.

Problem Number Three—Not-So-Fully Committed

This proposal contains another empty phrase we want to discuss. Consider this sentence: "It is important to note that our board is fully committed to the proposed project." In storytelling, showing is better than telling. In grantwriting, it is better to demonstrate the board's commitment rather than simply stating that they are committed. It is important for potential funders to know what specific steps the board has taken toward the presentation of a textile exhibition and whether they have made a financial contribution and if so, how much? Providing such specifics strengthens the case for support.

Problem Number Four—Too Long

Length. Because there are so many extraneous words and phrases, this is too long. When printed on 8½-by-11 paper with a one-inch margin, it fills two-and-a-half pages. As you'll see in the "after" version, this proposal can be condensed to about half of the space—without sacrificing the content.

Problem Number Five—Over and Over Again

Redundancies. Frequently and all too often, overly written is also redundantly written. (Looks as if we've caught a case of this ourselves!) In the "ugly duckling" example, CALM's founders are described as "feverishly passionate," the building they purchased was "run down and dilapidated," and the projected increase in attendance is "wonderfully glorious." A sharp editing pencil would eliminate these redundancies, leaving a crisper read.

Problem Number Six—Perception

Perception. We deliberately decided to use a fictitious arts organization to illustrate the problem of florid writing. In the grantseeking field, there is a recurring perception that artists, other than literary artists, are not the best communicators. Says Liesel Fenner of the New England Foundation for the Arts, "Artists (visual) often perpetuate the stereotype that they can't write. It saddens me when I see great ideas poorly communicated—artists reduce their chances of receiving a grant."

Poorly written proposals are not the exclusive domain of arts organizations. We have seen bad proposals from all types of nonprofit agencies—from environmental groups to educational institutions, from health care organizations to social service agencies. Our goal in this chapter is to give every grantwriter helpful hints for keeping flowery words and phrases out of their proposals. But arts agencies must face the perception that they are especially susceptible to writing poor proposals.

> **GRANTWRITING TIP!**
> Given the commonly held perception that arts organizations are especially prone to writing poor proposals, arts agencies should take extra care with their grantwriting.

POSITIVE COMMENTS

On the positive side, facts have not been lost to floridity in this example. Relevant facts and data are included, although sometimes hidden among the weedy verbiage. The reader is given the operating budget, the estimated budget to mount the textile exhibit, the number of pieces in the CALM collection, and actual and projected attendance figures and survey results, among others. This information helps present a strong case for the agency, though it is buried under a mountain of adjectives!

Florid writing can be corrected. If you're prone to this type of writing style, you'll either have to develop into a disciplined editor or run your drafts past someone who is. Let's look at some of the adjectives and adverbs from the "before" proposal and see if the copy can be made into something much cleaner and tighter.

**Community Art and Literacy Museum
Proposal to the Noel Norton Foundation for
Tactile Textiles: A Sensory Experience Exhibit**

CALM's Mission and 15-Year History

The Community Art and Literacy Museum (CALM) is one of Tranquil County's premier cultural resources, dedicated to showcasing the fine arts and literary works of local artists and writers. Our mission is "to enlighten and inspire the Tranquil County community by providing a venue for local artists."

Located in a 10,000-square-foot restored Beaux Arts building on Taupe Town's Main Square, CALM houses an impressive permanent collection of more than 600 paintings, sculptures, ceramics, and multi-media works—all created by renowned regional artists, such as Mike L. Angelo, Pablo P. Casio, and Vincent Van Go. CALM also serves as a vibrant hub of literary activity, as it offers an ongoing series of poetry and short story readings and houses the offices of *Simple Words,* an internationally renowned literary magazine.

CALM was founded in 1990 by a group of passionate arts patrons, including art collector Poindexter Moneybags. Early in the group's discussions, Mr. Poindexter committed to donating his sizable collection of contemporary Tranquil County art, provided a permanent site could be found for display of the collection. The Moneybags family had collected art for two generations yet had no means to publicly display its collection. With the Moneybags art collection as a catalyst, the founding group was able to raise more than $2M from local families and individuals during a three-year period. This funding enabled them to purchase and renovate the building that was to become CALM's home.

Today, the museum has an annual average attendance of 100,000 and employs 14 full-time and 6 part-time employees. Assisting the staff are dozens of dedicated volunteers who work as docents, provide additional administrative support, and help at various special events.

Since 1992, Pinkie Starr has served as CALM's Executive Director. Ms. Starr has a solid background in arts administration, having held senior administrative positions at the Louvre, the Museum of Modern Art, and the Getty Museum before joining CALM. Governance is provided by a diverse 15-member board of directors, which includes art patrons, businesspersons, lawyers, and experts in accounting, advertising, and marketing. One-third of the board members are people of color and eight are women. Board giving has a 100% participation rate, with cumulative support of nearly $100,000 annually. This year, CALM's operating budget is $2.1M with revenue coming from the following sources: admissions fees (50%), grants and individual gifts (25%), unrelated business income (15%), rental fees (9%), and earned interest (1%).

Tactile Textiles: A Sensory Experience: CALM's Proposed Exhibit

Visitors can view a variety of art forms at CALM, which *Art Museum Quarterly* named "one of the finest art museums in the state." Yet last year, more than 50% of CALM's visitors who responded to a written survey noted that they would "very much" like to see the museum either add textiles to its permanent collection or hold a textile exhibition. CALM's board of directors and administrative team considered this feedback, found it had merit, and began considering the options. They concluded that sponsoring a textile exhibition was the most feasible and economical alternative.

Opening in December 2007, CALM will present *Tactile Textiles: A Sensory Experience* in collaboration with Tranquil County Textile Artisans Association (TCTAA), a collective of weavers and other artisans. More than 100 exquisite pieces, including fabrics, garments, carpets, quilts, and other cloth items, will be displayed during the four-month run.

Based on attendance figures from other similar exhibitions nationwide, CALM conservatively estimates a 150% increase in visitors during the 120-day exhibition, which means an additional 16,000 visitors in 2007. In addition to repeat visits by local residents, CALM anticipates drawing many first-time visitors from out of the area. CALM intends to capitalize on the increased attendance with a targeted campaign to bolster museum memberships by at least 30%. New memberships provide CALM with immediate financial gains and with an opportunity for long-term financial support through membership renewals and donations. In addition to boosting museum attendance and memberships, *Tactile Textiles* will also have a positive economic impact on the local business community, specifically those businesses that rely on tourism, such as hotels, restaurants, and retail shops.

The board of directors fully endorses the presentation of the textile exhibit and the submission of this grant proposal. To provide financial leadership for this project, board members have collectively pledged $50,000.

CALM now seeks the sponsorship of local foundations and corporations to mount this visually stunning exhibition. The proposed budget for *Tactile Textiles,* which includes curatorial expenses, additional insurance, and promotional activities, is $425,000, of which CALM plans to raise $350,000 from foundations and corporations.

> Attached to this proposal is a list of the special benefits for the corresponding donor levels. We hope that the Noel Norton Foundation will consider a grant at the $50,000 level.

FLORID PROPOSAL MAKEOVER: STRONGER MESSAGE, FEWER WORDS

The benefits of a no-nonsense editing pencil are obvious. The flowery language from the before version has been judiciously pruned. Mind you, not every descriptive word or phrase has been eliminated. Enough have been retained to give the proposal some zest, some color.

For example, the description of the museum's permanent collection has been reworked from this:

"Today, CALM houses a permanent collection of more than 600 *magnificent* paintings (oil, acrylic and watercolor), sculptures, ceramics, and multi-media works from Tranquil County artists, thereby showcasing the *amazing* talent of our local artists"

to this:

"CALM houses an *impressive* permanent collection of more than 600 paintings, sculptures, ceramics, and multi-media works—all created by *renowned* regional artists, such as . . ."

Further, the gushing description of CALM Executive Director Pinkie Starr has been markedly improved from this:

"Pinkie Starr is CALM's *intelligent and resourceful* Executive Director and she has performed *marvelously* since her hiring in 1992"

to this:

"Ms. Starr has a solid background in arts administration, having held senior positions at . . ."

The edited version lets Ms. Starr's experience speak for itself. It is evident that during her tenure, the museum has been financially sound, built a loyal patron base, and delivered on its mission of providing a venue for local artists. A statement that the executive director has "performed marvelously" does not bolster the case. In fact, it may make the reader wonder whether she really did! This also sounds as if Ms. Starr is boasting, because she is likely to be the person submitting the proposal.

However, it is not an empty boast that the board of directors endorses the project, approves the submission of the proposal, and is also making a significant financial commitment with a pledge of $50,000. As noted earlier in the chapter, it is much stronger to provide such specific details rather than make sweeping generalities.

Finally, editing also nicely cut down on the length, but without forfeiting content. We believe that this shorter version enhances the message by delivering it in a more succinct fashion.

FINISHING UP "FLORID"

This chapter discussed the common, yet rarely ever fatal, flaw of florid writing in a grant proposal. A flowery writing style can get in the way of delivering your case for support. Too many descriptive words and phrases can dilute their individual impact. For example, describing your agency and everything and everyone affiliated with it only in superlatives is an exaggeration and one that can cause a grantmaker to question your agency's credibility.

Flowery proposals are also almost always too long. Again, this dilutes the impact of your message. Brevity is a virtue in grantseeking. Keep 'em short. Make each word count. Like spices, a few well-placed adjectives and adverbs can go a long way. Use them in moderate doses and you'll create *awesome* proposals.

The "Mystery" Proposal
Making Sense of Nonsense

There are times when a thesaurus comes in handy. Some of those times are when you're writing a proposal. Maybe you can't think of just the right word to convey your intended meaning, and a thesaurus will help you find it. Or you may want to avoid repeating the same word again and again, and a thesaurus will give you some substitutes. But most of the time, you are better off using the terms and expressions you use in everyday conversation when you are writing proposals. In other words, don't use ten-dollar words when fifty-cent words do a better job of telling your story.

In the previous chapter, "Florid Writing: When Proposals Go Over the Top," we addressed the problem of too many adjectives and adverbs—that is, florid writing. In this chapter, we tackle the related issues of writing that is abstract, vague, and academic and writing that uses a lot of jargon.

The trouble with a writing style that is academic or uses ten-dollar words is that the language is often unfamiliar and sometimes abstract. What may sound noble to your ear can come across as pompous or—worse yet—can leave the reader in the dark about what you really mean. You know the kind of language we mean: words like *interface* when you mean *relate*, *indigent* when you mean *poor* or *low-income*, *metamorphose* when you mean *change*, *finalize* when you mean *finish*.

Worse yet, once you get started down this path, it's easy to gather steam until you've strung together entire paragraphs of abstract or academic concepts and lost your reader entirely.

How about the following for a group's mission statement? "Superior Institution supports an educational process to increase problem visibility through group interaction. By channeling the latent capacities for strength among group members, we expect to harness the power to create a shift toward a sustainable economy." If you wonder what this group does, you're not alone. And if a grantmaker can't figure out what you do after reading your proposal, it's probably reached the end of the line.

A related problem is jargon. Too often, proposal writers try to impress the reader with their superior knowledge of the topic and their command of its unique language. As Aaron Jacobs of Social Venture Partners Seattle says, "Jargon is annoying; big words when little will do is annoying."

Unfortunately, the more sophisticated or cerebral your vocabulary, the less it may say about what you really do. In fact, sometimes these big words are really just a front for fuzzy thinking. When funders see sentences like "Bridge to Maturity helps youth with complex challenges discover their full potential through an array of integrated services by synthesizing our program to offer a unique opportunity for our students to learn, grow, and succeed," they might suspect that the writer isn't quite sure what Bridge to Maturity actually does—and they might be right.

This kind of writing is all too common according to the grantmakers we surveyed. Lori McGlinchey of Open Society Institute states, "The most common bad writing style is vague, overblown, indirect language." In fact, "academic, vague language" was cited more frequently than any other writing style as annoying by survey respondents, with 78 percent citing this as a pet peeve.

Take a look at this proposal from a fictitious inner-city high school. It starts off all right, but before too long it gets bogged down in a mire of abstract words and concepts.

**High School of Hard Knocks
Proposal to the Too Good to Be True Foundation
for the New Horizons Initiative**

The High School of Hard Knocks (HSoHK) in Urban City offers a profoundly superior but affordable educational alternative to inner-city youth ages 14 to 18. Our aim is to provide students who have been low-performing with an array of educational services integrated with a unique curriculum to help them attain the qualities and skills they need for successful adult life and to realize their full potential. The school opened three years ago with our first class of 50 freshmen. Our enrollment is now 250 and in June the first class of 41 students will graduate.

We are seeking funding for a new academic component to further our mission of "preparing tomorrow's Urban City citizens." The total cost for the "New Horizons Initiative" is $75,000 for the first year, and I am writing today to ask the Too Good to Be True Foundation to consider a grant for this amount. I believe you will find the benefits to be worth the investment of your funding.

The Need

At HSoHK we believe that our youth are our future and we are determined to invest them with the skills and attributes they need for a bright future. The youth we serve face multiple challenges to their future success. Nearly all reside in the southeast sector of Urban City, an area marked by high rates of indigence. 70% of the population is low-income according to the latest census and local schools report that 86% of the students qualify for free or reduced price lunches.

Most of our students attended local public schools prior to their enrollment at HSoHK. Unfortunately, as with many of the schools in

Urban City, these schools are notable for their crumbling infrastructure, the mismanagement of their scant resources and the resulting poor performance of their students on standardized tests.

In fact, two of the local elementary schools were closed recently because of fiscal mismanagement and the junior high has been threatened with closure unless student performance improves. As a result many students are being bussed to other neighborhoods to attend school and are losing touch with their community and their culture. If the junior high school also closes, all teens attending public schools will be bussed outside the community.

For the most part our students come to us unprepared for the challenging academic and social environment of high school. According to our intake assessments, most are three to four years behind their grade level in verbal skills and lag two or more years in math/science.

At the same time the community has several notable assets. Family structures are sound and parents share a strong commitment to their children's education. 60% of the students come from two-parent families—an unusually high percentage in any population—and the local schools have among the highest participation rates in PTA activities. While most adults are employed in low-paying jobs, there is a strong work ethic and many work several jobs to support their families.

Our goal at HSoHK is to bring students up to grade level by their junior year and provide them with marketable skills so they will have real choices for employment or continuing their education at graduation. We accomplish this through a rigorous academic program. Our students attend classes seven and a half hours every weekday and half days every other Saturday. Support for improvement in academic outcomes is available for students who need it.

We have been successful in meeting our objectives thus far. But we find that our students' vision for their future is limited by unfamiliarity with viable careers and by a lack of appropriate role models. At the same time, parents continue to be concerned that students are losing touch with their own culture and are not motivated to give back to their community.

New Horizons Initiative: Goals

Working collaboratively with the local Private Industry Council (PIC) and local social and cultural groups, we have designed the New Horizons Initiative to address these issues. Our goals are:

- To expand students horizons for future success.
- To increase students critical thinking and leadership skills.
- To provide ingress for students to local intellectual and cultural capital.

Methodology

We have worked with the PIC (Private Industry Council) and others to develop a careful plan and budget for the initiative. (The participants in this collaborative effort are listed in Attachment 3.) By harnessing the dynamism of relevant cultural icons we can crystallize the values we seek. Students will be enrolled in the initiative in the second semester of their sophomore year. This is about the time when most HSoHK students are catching up academically and ready for new challenges. It also allows students to participate in two summer sessions, one following their sophomore year and the second after their junior year. The program will run year-round and will serve 150 students, 75 from HSoHK and 75 from the local community through a balanced "outreach and in-reach" technological marketing methodology. This will allow us to create the nexus for arming emerging community leaders with the facility to be powerful motivators for the social good.

We will hire a full-time project coordinator for the project and plan to recruit a young adult from the local community for this position. Working with an advisory council made up of the collaboration members, the coordinator will design the specific project activities. Activities will be designed to interface with the rigorous academic curriculum, aimed at achieving the goals stated above and reflective of our high standards of excellence in pedagogy and tutelage. The syllabus will be tailored to meet the unique needs of each individual participant, but it will also focus on group dynamics and group outcomes. By demonstrating the correlation between success in school and success in life, the New Horizons Initiative will encompass a new vision for Urban City's future—one that nurtures excellence and rewards future development efforts.

We are deeply committed to utilizing local intellectual and creative capital to achieve systemic change and plan to address fundamentals that will provide students with currency in the world of responsible adults. This will metamorphose to accountability for enforced outcomes for each student and for each cohort. By drawing on local resources, the program will reinforce cultural and social assets in the students' community and re-integrate them to the values of their heritage. In this way, students will reclaim the strengths and values of their culture and give voice to their unique and shared talents.

Aside from the project coordinator, all other staffing will be by volunteers.

Expected Outcomes and Evaluation

Our primary expected outcome is systemic change in the local cultural milieu; specifically, the entire community will be empowered to encourage the success of our students. Evaluation will be ongoing. We will seek feedback from students, peers, teachers, parents and members of the collaborative.

Further, the New Horizons Initiative will incorporate an innovative, comprehensive evaluation method. This quasi-experimental evaluation design addresses process, outcome, and impact evaluation questions, and provides a self-correcting feedback mechanism for program participants and managers to use in monitoring and adjusting the program during its implementation.

Future Funding

The local PIC has made a significant in-kind contribution to this project, as have local cultural and social agencies. Once success has been demonstrated we will launch an extensive fundraising campaign aimed at our major donors and at local businesses.

Conclusion

A review of the guidelines and annual report of the Too Good to Be True Foundation has convinced us that your trustees share our commitment to youth as the future of our community. The New Horizons Initiative matches the goals of the Foundation's Educational Innovations funding category. New Horizons will be a significant enhancement to the curriculum at Hard Knocks. Our school is already recognized as an institutional treasure in our community. We invite your eleemosynary investment in our efforts to prepare youth to take their place as contributing adult citizens in Urban City.

WHAT'S IT ALL ABOUT?

What's wrong with this proposal? The High School of Hard Knocks sounds like a worthy institution serving a population that can really benefit from the education they provide. It also looks like the school has been successful in helping students improve their academic performance. Likewise the concept of the school's New Horizons Initiative—to get students to raise their sights in terms of future academic and career goals—seems like a good idea, and Hard Knocks is probably the right organization for the job.

In addition to a few overblown words and phrases and the use of the acronym HSoHK, which is hard to read, the first hint of serious trouble comes with the project's goals. Though these appear to be noble, they are also more than a trifle vague. As we make clear in Chapter Five, "Evaluation: Making Sure the Proposal Measures Up," good project goals point to obvious outcomes and methods for evaluating success. But how will the High School of Hard Knocks measure expanded horizons? Or increased critical thinking and leadership skills? The third goal (providing ingress to local intellectual and cultural capital) is downright mysterious.

But the writer really starts spinning a major mystery in a big way in the Methodology section. What activities will actually make up the program of New Horizons? We know who the planning partners are. We know the rationale for the timing of student enrollment in the middle of their sophomore year. But whatever is meant by "a balanced outreach and in-reach technological marketing methodology"? We know the program will be staffed by someone from the community and by volunteers. But what exactly will students do when they enroll in New Horizons? And who are the volunteers and what are their credentials? Can you tell from what is stated in the proposal?

There are a few clues. We're told that "activities will . . . interface with the rigorous academic curriculum," and a "syllabus" is mentioned. This points to an academic component. From the mention of "group dynamics and group process," some group activities seem likely. And the mention of cultural heritage hints at a cultural component. But readers will be left with more questions than answers after reading this proposal. And potential grantmakers should not have to rely on hints and hunches to determine how their money is going to be spent. The specific program components of the New Horizons Initiative remain a mystery. When asked to name her pet peeve in poorly written proposals, Anne Vally of The James

Irvine Foundation responded, "Proposals that are full of jargon and don't explain, in plain language, what the organization would do with proposed funds."

> **GRANTWRITING TIP!**
> Don't risk confusing or irritating a prospective funder.
> Try to anticipate questions about your project and
> answer them in your proposal.

WARNING: LOFTY VOCABULARY AND NOBLE PHRASES MAY BE HARMFUL TO YOUR CAUSE!

What's more, the writer of this proposal is straining a little too hard to impress the reader with high-sounding phrases and a lofty vocabulary. The sentence "By harnessing the dynamism of relevant cultural icons we can crystallize the values we seek," is meaningless. Noble-sounding but equally meaningless is "This will allow us to create the nexus for arming emerging community leaders with the facility to be powerful motivators for the social good." As Elizabeth M. Lynch of the Massachusetts Bar Foundation points out, "Proposals filled with NGO-speak, buzz words, and the latest catch phrases are sometimes utterly incomprehensible."

By the time we get down to the Expected Outcomes and Evaluation, the writer has hit full stride. Here we encounter the noble phrases "systemic change in the local cultural milieu" and the impressive-sounding "quasi-experimental evaluation design," which is "innovative," to boot!

Unfortunately, grantmakers are not likely to be impressed. In fact, most of them probably won't read all the way down to the conclusion, where they can encounter the use of "eleemosynary investment" to describe their possible grant! (Don't run to your dictionaries. *Eleemosynary* simply means *charitable* or *philanthropic,* two perfectly descriptive words that are understood by everyone.) Rather, proposal reviewers will be left wondering just what the program is about. Worse yet, they may be feeling somewhat uneasy. Perhaps they are wondering what fuzzy thinking and poor planning is being obscured by this onslaught of lofty words and abstract concepts.

Can this proposal be saved? What can be done to rescue it from terminal intellectualism? When we teach proposal writing, we often advise students to pretend they are explaining their organization or project to a family member or friend over the phone. What would you say? Most of us don't use words like "eleemosynary" or phrases like "harnessing the dynamism of relevant cultural icons" in our everyday conversation. Remember that the purpose of a proposal is to communicate, not to impress.

GRANTWRITING TIP!
Write as you speak!

EXTREME MAKEOVER AHEAD

Let's take a look at a rewrite of the proposal from the High School of Hard Knocks.

**High School of Hard Knocks
Proposal to the Too Good to Be True Foundation
for the New Horizons Initiative**

Introduction

The High School of Hard Knocks in Urban City offers a superior but affordable educational alternative to inner-city youth ages 14 to 18. Our aim is to provide students who have been low performing with a well-rounded education to help them attain the qualities and skills they need for successful adult life. The school opened three years ago, with our first class of 50 freshmen. Our enrollment is now 250, and in June the first class of 41 students will graduate.

We are seeking funding for a new academic component to further our mission of "preparing tomorrow's Urban City citizens." The total cost for the New Horizons Initiative is $75,000 for the first year, and I am writing today to ask the Too Good to Be True Foundation to consider a grant for this amount.

The Need

At Hard Knocks, we believe that our youth are our future. The young people we serve face multiple challenges to their success. Nearly all reside in the southeast sector of Urban City—an area marked by high poverty rates. 70% of the population is low-income according to the latest census, and local schools report that 86% of the students qualify for free or reduced-price lunches.

Most of our students attended local public schools prior to their enrollment at Hard Knocks. Unfortunately, as with many of the schools in Urban City, these schools are notable for their crumbling infrastructure, the mismanagement of their scant resources, and the resulting poor performance of their students on standardized tests.

In fact, two of the local elementary schools were closed recently because of fiscal mismanagement, and the junior high has been threatened with closure unless student performance improves. As a result, many students are being bussed to other neighborhoods to attend school and are losing touch with their community and their culture. If the junior high school also closes, all teens attending public schools will be bussed outside the community.

For the most part, our students come to us unprepared for the challenging academic and social environment of high school. According to our intake assessments, most are three to four years behind their grade level in verbal skills and lag two or more years in math/science.

At the same time, the community has several notable assets. Family structures are generally sound, and parents share a strong commitment to their children's education. 60% of the students come from two-parent families—an unusually high percentage in any population—and the local schools have among the highest participation rates in PTA activities. Even though most adults are employed in low-paying jobs, there is a strong work ethic, and many work several jobs to support their families.

Our goal at Hard Knocks is to bring students up to grade level by their junior year and provide them with marketable skills, so they will have real choices for employment or continuing their education at graduation. We accomplish this through a rigorous academic program. Our students attend classes seven and a half hours every weekday and half days every other Saturday. Extra tutorial help is also available for students who need it.

We have been successful in meeting our objectives thus far. But we find that our students' vision for their future is limited—by unfamiliarity with viable careers and by a lack of appropriate role models. At the same time, parents are concerned that students are losing touch with their own culture and its values.

New Horizons Initiative: Goals

Working collaboratively with the local Private Industry Council (PIC) and local social and cultural groups, we have designed the New Horizons Initiative to address these issues. Our goal is to expand students' horizons for future success by increasing their critical thinking and leadership skills and strengthening their connections within their own community and culture.

Our objectives for the New Horizons Initiative for the first year are:

- To improve the academic performance of 150 participating high school students as measured by grade point averages.
- To broaden their expectations of possible future careers.
- To strengthen their identification with their culture of origin and to create an appreciation and respect for other cultures.
- To instill the expectation of "giving back to community" as part of their value system.

Methodology

We have worked with the PIC (Private Industry Council) and others to develop a careful plan and budget for the initiative. The participants in this collaborative effort are listed in Attachment 3 and include local cultural organizations representing the various ethnic groups in our community in addition to the PIC. By partnering with these groups,

New Horizons will offer culturally appropriate programming and role models for participants.

Students will be enrolled in the initiative in the second semester of their sophomore year. This is about the time when most Hard Knocks students are catching up academically and ready for new challenges. It also allows students to participate in two summer sessions—one following their sophomore year and the second after their junior year. In addition to an intensive nine-week core program during the summer, the program will run year-round, with twice monthly Saturday group sessions and individual work. It will serve 150 students, 75 from Hard Knocks and 75 from the local community. Hard Knocks students will be recruited through our Web site, through presentations to students and our parent group, and through e-mails sent through our schoolwide network. Other students who do not attend Hard Knocks will be recruited by the cultural organizations we are partnering with. Balancing participation by Hard Knocks students with students from other high schools will forge strong community alliances and build community leadership.

We will hire a full-time project coordinator for the project and plan to recruit a young adult from the local community for this position. Working with an advisory council made up of the collaboration members, the coordinator will design the specific project activities to include the following:

- *Academic Component:* remedial math, English, communications, and so forth through the formation of peer study groups. This component will feature cooperative learning.
- *Career Component:* exploration of career options through presentations by successful working adults from the local community and

through internships with local businesses and organizations. The PIC will recruit volunteers who are engaged in skilled labor and white-collar industries to make presentations on their careers. The PIC and local cultural organizations will provide internship placements. This component will stress the correlation between success in school and success in life and will provide role models to emulate.

- *Service Component:* volunteer opportunities and internships with local agencies. This component will demonstrate the value of "giving back."
- *Cultural Component:* presentations by partner cultural organizations and visits to local cultural institutions. This component will teach both the value of each student's culture or origin and respect for other cultures.
- *Group Project Component:* in small groups, students will work on a career, service, or cultural project of their choosing. This component will teach group dynamics, consensus building, and teamwork.

Aside from the project coordinator, all other staffing will be by volunteers. The PIC will recruit and train adult role models for the Career Component. Cultural organizations and nonprofit agencies will staff the Cultural and Service Components. Hard Knocks teachers will act as moderators for the Academic Component and advisors to student groups in the Group Project Component.

Expected Outcomes and Evaluation

Rather than conduct evaluation only at the end of the year, evaluation will be ongoing. Program activity, enrollment, and attendance records will provide data on whether the program is meeting process objectives: Did enrollment meet expectations? Did activities take place as planned? How many attended? By monitoring students' grades, we can measure academic outcomes. We will also seek feedback via online questionnaires from students, peers, teachers, parents, and members of the collaborative at least every other month and will tabulate and share results with all parties. This *continuous feedback loop* is meant to provide positive reinforcement for desired outcomes and an opportunity to adjust the program when expectations are not met.

By using online survey instruments, we can easily automate tabulation of results. Survey questions will address:

- Outcome (What was learned?)
- Impact (What has changed?)
- Quality (Did it meet your need and expectations? What would you change or add?)

Future Funding

The local PIC has made a significant in-kind contribution to this project, as have local cultural and social agencies. Once success has been demonstrated, we will launch an extensive fundraising campaign aimed at our major donors and at local businesses.

Conclusion

A review of the guidelines and annual report of the Too Good to Be True Foundation has convinced us that your trustees share our commitment to youth as the future of our community. The New Horizons Initiative matches the goals of the Foundation's Educational Innovations funding category. Our school is already recognized as an institutional treasure in our community. New Horizons will be a significant enhancement of the curriculum at Hard Knocks, as well as a substantial new resource for other youth in our community. We invite your investment in our efforts to prepare youth to take their place as contributing adult citizens in Urban City.

MYSTERY SOLVED!

Other than eliminating the use of the HSoHK acronym and making a few word changes to tone down the vocabulary—for instance, the hyperbole of "profoundly superior" in the first paragraph becomes just plain "superior" in the new version—the substantive changes begin with the project objectives. In addition to being more specific and measurable, the objectives give a better indication of the evaluation methods to be employed. They also point to some obvious program components. It's clear now that there will be an academic and a cultural component. It's also clear that career exploration and community service will be part of the program.

But the really big changes are in the Methodology. We're given more details on the schedule for the program—a nine-week summer program, Saturday sessions, and independent work by students—and the mystery of that "outreach and in-reach technological marketing methodology" is also solved, with a plain and simple description of the methods that will be used to attract and enroll students. The bulleted list of the program components goes a long way toward solving the "mystery" of the original proposal. How volunteers will fit into the staffing plan is also clarified.

There are also significant changes in Expected Outcomes and Evaluation. In fact, little remains of the old proposal in this section. Instead the writer has stated clearly what methods will be used to gather program data and results and what questions will be addressed.

SUMMING UP: CRYSTAL CLEAR COMMUNICATION

Together with a clear budget, a well-written proposal reassures prospective funders by letting them know exactly how their money will be spent and what they can expect in terms of outcomes. All of us enjoy reading a good mystery from time to time, but a grant proposal is not the time to try your hand at this literary genre. Don't keep your reader in the dark about what you plan to do! Remember that your goal is communication. Plain language and a clear, direct writing style will work best to communicate your project and your organization.

As Grace Caliendo of the John Muir/Mt. Diablo Community Health Fund puts it, "You will really get someone's attention if you make it easy for them to understand what you do—how does it translate into action?"

The Perfect Package

Preparing a proposal for submission is a lot like getting ready for the prom. There are many choices and decisions to make. There's much primping and preening. Ultimately, you want to look cool. The same is true with a grant proposal. You want yours to stand out from the crowd—and for the right reasons.

In this chapter, we'll discuss how to package your proposal—from font size to formatting, from the use of bold and italics to charts and graphs. This is the makeover "dress for success" chapter. It covers all those technical questions you worry about after you've written that terrifically compelling narrative.

WHAT TO PUT ON THE BLANK PAGE

Let's begin with a blank page. This is what proposals are printed on. White 8½-by-11 paper. Not your agency's letterhead. No fancy colored stock. Just plain old bond. James R. Posner of the Posner-Wallace Foundation recommends that "there must be wide enough margins to hang onto the edge with your finger." Set 1-inch margins all around. This creates the canvas for your creative work in writing a masterpiece proposal.

We use a 12-point typeface, which is what the vast majority of our survey respondents prefer. "This ensures that your proposal will be easy to read, especially for the reviewer who has been reading 10-point text all day!" says Elizabeth M. Lynch of the Massachusetts Bar Foundation.

"A longer proposal is preferred to one that has a really small font," explains Anne Vally of the James Irvine Foundation.

A few program officers noted that 10-point type was the minimum acceptable size—and we suspect that they are young and still have keen eyesight. Our preference is a larger type size to ensure readability.

Because readability is crucial, we also select a clean, straightforward typeface, such as Times New Roman, Arial, or similar fonts, for a grant proposal is not the document in which to experiment with fanciful fonts that evoke William Shakespeare's quill pen.

Perhaps Janice Ashbury of the J. W. McConnell Family Foundation sums it up best when she says, "Fancy fonts don't help the understanding."

THE BUSY PAGE

Our advice, and that from our survey respondents, is *keep it simple.* This is true for typeface and font, as well as for other formatting elements, such as italics, bolding, bullets, and headings. According to our survey responses, program officers want to read proposals that are uncluttered by a multitude of different formatting devices. "Moderation" was the word used many times by program officers when it comes to formatting.

But the majority of funders do recommend the use of bold or italics (or both) in headings and subheads—and we agree. Readers need restful breaks in the copy, which headings and subheads provide, even more so when they are presented in bold or italics. But use these devices sparingly within the narrative text itself. It is often appropriate to emphasize a word or phrase by using bold or italics, but if you do so too many times, you'll lose the effect you were trying to achieve. There's one final point concerning presentation on the page: several program officers commented that numbering and bulleting are helpful in the body of a proposal to break up dense text and to improve the readability of the proposal.

"Simple formatting is helpful—the use of subheads, bullets, etc.," says Barbara Kemmis of the Crossroads Fund. "But complicated formatting with underlined text, bold and highlighted text, and multiple fonts is often distracting."

"It's distracting if there are too many elements," says Grace Caliendo of the John Muir/Mt. Diablo Community Health Fund.

"Please use one or maybe two fonts and limit the bold and italics to a minimum and where appropriate," advises Kathy Zundel of Sisters of Mercy of the Americas, St. Louis Regional Community.

"Don't overdo," cautions Adeeba Deterville of Citibank. "Have another reader look over the proposal to check for easy readability."

There's another compelling reason why one shouldn't overuse formatting options and fancy texts: online submissions. These days, a growing number of funders accept online requests. Some even require it. Unfortunately, elaborate formatting can get lost in electronic transmissions, and most likely you'll never know it. When transmission problems occur and your text is littered with computer symbols rather than recognizable words, the reader may have a more difficult time reviewing your proposal. For this reason and for those just outlined, we strongly recommend that you keep your formatting simple.

> **GRANTWRITING TIP!**
> Less really is more! Limit the number of different typefaces and fonts used in a proposal to one or two and go lightly on the use of bold and italics.

CHARTS, GRAPHS, AND PHOTOGRAPHS

What about the inclusion of charts, graphs, and photographs in the proposal narrative? Computer technology enables us to more easily add these to our proposals, but should we? On this issue, program officers are decidedly split.

Fifteen of the sixty-nine respondents gave a flat-out no to the inclusion of charts, graphs, and photographs within the narrative itself. Another half dozen respondents indicated that although they don't recommend or encourage the addition of charts, graphs, and photographs, they will allow them. "We do not recommend charts and graphs but recognize that they sometimes synthesize financial or evaluation information in useful ways," explains Frances Phillips of the Walter and Elise Haas Fund.

The remaining program officers favored the inclusion of such enhancements with varying degrees of enthusiasm.

Fifteen gave their unqualified endorsement. Says Sister Janet Burkhart, HM, of the Sisters of the Humility of Mary, "Whatever works for the applicant to make a coherent and persuasive case."

"Yes," says Mary Gregory of Pacific Foundation Services. "Especially to emphasize the target audience and community demographics for outreach."

And Mary Vallier-Kaplan of the Endowment for Health explains, "It depends on the project, but sometimes visuals can be the simplest way of explaining the project, and often a good photograph can be useful to share at a board meeting to help the board members understand and be moved by a program's work."

But the majority of those program officers who are willing to accept charts, graphs, and photographs noted that a grantwriter should include them only when these further the grantmaker's understanding of the applicant's request for funding.

"[Include these] only if that is the applicant's preferred way to tell their story," says Anne Vally of the James Irvine Foundation.

"If charts, graphs or photographs add significantly to the explanation of what the organization is trying to accomplish and how effective it is at reaching this impact, yes [include them]," says Barbara Kemmis of the Crossroads Foundation. "Usually, however, these additional elements aren't focused enough to add anything more to the narrative."

"Only if they are clearly understandable," says Christine Elbel of the Fleishhacker Foundation.

"A clear, concise narrative is preferred, but if charts, graphs and/or photographs help to illustrate a point, they're fine," says Barbara Silzie of the Leeway Foundation.

We're able to draw some important conclusions from the responses and comments of our survey respondents. First, find out what the preferences of the particular funder are. Typically, you'll find this information in the funder's guidelines or on their Web site. If a grantmaker specifically says that they do not want or encourage the inclusion of charts, graphs, and photographs in proposals, don't include them. Conversely, if a grantmaker encourages the submission of charts, graphs, and photographs, by all means, include them, but only if it makes sense for you to do so.

If a funder doesn't specify a preference, you may want to call and ask for guidance. Should you be unable to reach the funder or if they have no established policy, our advice is to use elements such as charts, graphs, and photographs sparingly—and only if they truly advance the presentation of your case for support.

When including charts and graphs, heed the advice of the program officers and make certain these extra elements enhance the reader's ability to understand the information being conveyed. As Carolyn Young of the Hogg Foundation for Mental Health advises, "Charts and graphs [are acceptable] if they present a cleaner presentation regarding data supporting the initiative, e.g., populations served, program performance, etc."

However, you don't need to include charts, graphs, and photographs simply because today's technology makes it possible to do so. Finally, keep in mind that if you are submitting online, you may run the risk of losing such formatting devices in the transmission.

> **GRANTWRITING TIP!**
>
> Funders are split over the use of charts, graphs, and photographs in proposals. If possible, find out the funder's preference before including one or more of these elements. If you use these devices, make certain that they are relevant, provide useful information, and truly advance your agency's case for support.

GOT ATTACHMENTS?

The final step in proposal preparation is deciding what attachments to include. Our advice is to send only those items that the funder wants and nothing more. You won't get extra points by adding additional items to the package.

Respondents to our survey back us up. Donna Gassie of the Virginia Tobacco Settlement Fund says to enclose "just what we ask for," and Karen Topakian of the Agape Foundation says, "We don't require attachments and we like them kept to a minimum."

For those funders that request attachments, what are they looking for? The usual list of attachments includes your agency's 501(c)(3) letter, a list of the agency's board of directors, your agency's overall annual budget, and audited financial statements. Let's take a closer look at each of these standard attachments before considering some of the other items specific funders might request.

501(c)(3) Letter

Issued by the Internal Revenue Service, this documents the fact that your agency has not-for-profit status. This is pretty straightforward. Either your agency has its own 501(c)(3) designation or it doesn't. If it does not yet have its own 501(c)(3) designation, or if the application for one with the IRS is pending, your agency may have a fiscal sponsor, which means that it "uses" the tax-exempt status of another not-for-profit agency. In such situations, you would submit a copy of your fiscal sponsor's 501(c)(3) letter. If your agency has its 501(c)(3) letter, we suggest that you make a dozen or more photocopies so you have them readily on hand for proposal submissions. Put the original letter in a safe place so you can find it when you need to make additional copies.

Board of Directors List

Grantmakers are interested in knowing the composition of your agency's board of directors, so they request a list of board members. Typically, this means a list of board member names and occupations or affiliations. For example, "Tyrone Ferguson, Fundraising Consultant" or "Dorotea Argueta, Vice President, Urban City Bank."

There are several reasons why funders want to see this information. First, they often want to see if the board reflects the community or the constituents being served. For example, an agency in the health care field should have at least some medically trained professionals (physicians, nurses, medical technicians, and the like) on the board of directors. Second, an agency's credibility can be enhanced or even established by the composition of the board. A brand-new agency becomes more credible in the eyes of a potential funder if it has attracted individuals who bring to the board expertise in the agency's area of operations or who are well connected to community movers and shakers.

Consequently, if Fred Boyd is listed as simply *retired* on the board of directors list for a community health care clinic when he's actually a retired M.D. and the former chief of staff at a local hospital, the agency has missed an important opportunity to "show its stuff." Similarly, if a board member is also the parent of a child enrolled in an agency program, the organization would be advised to say so.

In addition to the "name, rank, and serial number" board member information, some grantmakers ask for more.

Randy Okamura of SBC wants not only a list of board members but their biographies as well. Aaron Jacobs of Social Venture Partners wants to see the number of years each board member has served.

Sister Janet Burkhart, HM, of Sisters of the Humility of Mary looks "for the presence of women, and when possible, we also look for the presence of minorities as well as people who would be impacted."

Audited Financial Statements

Because grantmakers want to understand the financial health of the applicant agency, they will often request enclosure of the agency's most recent audited financial statements. Typically, nonprofit agencies with annual budgets of about $250,000 or more will engage a CPA to undertake and prepare an annual audit. This is an examination and evaluation of an agency's accounting practices, as well as a verification of the accuracy of the financial numbers reported by the agency. Small-budget agencies are less likely to incur the expense of an audit, and funders will often waive the requirement that they submit audited financial statements. However, we encourage smaller organizations to include their most recent year-end balance sheet, along with their current income and expense statement, in order to satisfy the requirements of most funders.

TO ATTACH OR NOT TO ATTACH

Your agency's 501(c)(3) letter, board of directors list, and audited financial statements (whenever possible) are the attachments most often requested by funders. In addition to these usual attachments, grantmakers may ask applicants to provide numerous other items. When any of the following are requested, make certain that you enclose them. Other attachments may include a board resolution authorizing the submission of the proposal; a copy of the agreement or memorandum of understanding if the program is a collaboration; letters of support; a time line; a copy of the agency's strategic plan; resume, curriculum vitae, or background information on the staff managing the project; the publicity plan; results of previous evaluations; and a logic model for evaluation.

You may be surprised to see that a few items are not included in this list, specifically an agency brochure, newsletter, news clippings, videos, and CDs. Generally, funders expect a proposal to be complete and answer all of their questions. The information found in brochures, newsletters, videos, CDs, and the like should not be adding anything new to a well-written, comprehensive proposal narrative, and therefore we typically do not include them with our submissions.

In fact, funders frequently discourage the inclusion of such items with your submission for very practical reasons. First, there's the duplicating issue. At many foundations and corporations, the very first step taken with your submission is to make photocopies, which are then distributed to one or more reviewers. But what happens to your brochure, newsletter, video, and CD? The funder usually does not have the ability to reproduce these items (much less view a video while reading proposals on a commuter bus!). Often those materials will be placed in a file never again to see the light of day.

For this reason as well as environmental ones, funders generally discourage the use of binders and folders with proposal submissions. Binders and folders also make it difficult for the funder to photocopy your proposal.

The second issue concerning the enclosure of additional optional attachments is storage. Funders simply do not have the capacity to store brochures, newsletters, videos, and CDs. When packaging your proposal, it is best to leave these materials out; however, you can tell the funder you have such items and offer to send them at a later date if the funder so chooses.

Mary Gregory of Pacific Foundation Services explains, "Usually, I hope that the proposal narrative contains the information I need, but occasionally I have relied on information contained in a brochure or newsletter. To me, that's not the best way, though. You don't want program officers to have to hunt for information they need.

"Only send a newspaper clipping if it's the best written and most succinct piece you have that demonstrates your program's operation—otherwise write the case study yourself from an actual client story," adds Mary Gregory.

FINAL PACKAGING POINTS

The appropriate packaging of a grant proposal is much like putting the proper punctuation mark at the end of a sentence: You don't have a complete sentence without one. Similarly, you won't have a complete proposal unless you pay attention to details like typeface, font size, formatting, and attachments. Whenever possible, find out if the grantmaker has any preferences about such items. If so, follow the funder's recommendations to the letter. If the funder is silent on such matters, then rely on common sense, and you should have the perfectly packaged proposal.

PACKAGING CHECKLIST

To sum it all up, here's a helpful checklist:

- Use one-inch margins on plain bond paper for your proposals, not fancy colored stock.

- Preferred type size is 12 point or larger (minimum is 10 point) in a standard font, such as Times New Roman or Arial.

- Use of italics, bold, bullets, and headings can enhance readability, but don't overdo! Go for the uncluttered look.

- Use charts, graphs, and photos sparingly and only if they will really make it easier to understand your proposal.

- Send only the attachments the funder requests. Standard attachments are your agency's IRS 501(c)(3) letter, board list (showing affiliations), financial statements (audited, if possible), and budgets.

- Refrain from including things like videos, CDs, newsletters, fancy folders, or binders—in short, anything that is not easily photocopied, because it is usually a waste of resources. Check with the funder before you send any of these.

MISSION ACCOMPLISHED: TRANSFORMATION COMPLETE

Editing. Rewriting. Improving. *Transforming.* Giving your proposals an effective makeover is challenging work. This we know from personal experience. Trial and error. Mistakes and successes. The value of hindsight. Guidance and wisdom offered by dozens of thoughtful program officers. Over the years, we've gleaned insights and learned valuable lessons that have sharpened our skills as grantwriters. We wrote this book to share our knowledge and help you become more successful in your grantseeking. We hope we've given you practical tips and useful information, so you can both build better proposals and transform mediocre ones.

We also hope you have come to realize, as we have, that writing successful proposals is as much an art as it is a science. There are opportunities for creative expression and for presenting your agency's case for support using your own unique voice. On many occasions, we have been asked whether there is a proposal template that writers can use as a guide. Even if there were such a thing as a universal proposal template, we would discourage its use, because a template cannot adequately or passionately convey the uniqueness of your agency and its case. Nor will it provide the unique information needed by each funder. This is the true art of grantwriting.

Yet there are also some hard and fast rules. Generally, the funders determine the rules of the grantmaking game, and playing by the rules will keep you in the game and give you the best chance of winning. Although there is much agreement among funders about what the rules are, there is also internal debate, differences of opinion, and occasional outright disagreement. By surveying a broad spectrum of grantmakers and incorporating their opinions and quotes throughout the previous chapters, we wanted you to see the major points of agreement as well as those areas where funders differ.

The reason for the differences and disagreements within the grantmaking community is really straightforward. As the saying goes, when you've seen one foundation, you've seen one foundation. They are all unique. Every grantmaking institution has its own philanthropic philosophy. Every grantmaking institution has its own preferences for how they want an applicant to approach them and what they want to see in a proposal. Furthermore, every program officer has his or her own individual preferences regarding both writing style and content.

What this means is: know your funder. This is the first rule of successful grantseeking. Take every opportunity and use all means available to learn everything you can about a prospective funder. Read the funder's guidelines, annual reports, Web site, and list of recent grantees. If the funder welcomes phone calls before the submission of a letter of inquiry or full proposal, be sure to call if you have any unanswered questions. This also gives you the perfect opportunity to initiate a relationship with the potential funder. Your knowledge of a particular grantmaker and that grantmaker's priorities and preferences will help you craft a proposal tailored to the funder and therefore more likely to stand out from the others in the pile on the program officer's desk.

Although "know your funder" is the most important rule, there are others that we covered in our book's preceding chapters. Here's a summary of the other key rules:

- Follow funder guidelines to the letter.
- Demonstrate that your agency and its programs are aligned with the funder's giving priorities.
- Make sure your proposals adhere to an organized structure.
- Thoroughly describe and document the problem or need being addressed.
- Let moderation be your watchword. If a startling statistic does a good job of helping to make your case, use it. But if one or two are good, this doesn't mean that ten or twenty are better. Same thing with charts and graphs or bulleted lists or boldface or . . . well, you get the idea.
- Articulate specific, measurable objectives and explain how you will track them through an evaluation system.

- Present thorough and clear budget information, being especially careful that the numbers add up and are consistent with what is said in the narrative.

- Brevity is a virtue. Include all the information needed for the funder to make a decision . . . and no more.

- Eliminate flowery, abstract, or pontificating language.

Follow the rules, use common sense, and add a dash of creativity. That's the basic recipe for success in grantseeking.

Our definition of success is the formation of a partnership between grantor and grantee to address challenges and problems in society, both large and small. The funder brings financial resources to the relationship. The nonprofit agency brings professional expertise and experience. By combining forces, truly great things are accomplished. Children are educated. Artistic visions become reality. Fragile environments are protected. Civil liberties are safeguarded. The list goes on and on.

We are proud to work in the nonprofit field, where so many good people are working to achieve great things for the common good. We wish you good fortune in finding the funders who share your vision and partnering with them to transform your corner of the world.

RESOURCE A: CHECKLIST FOR A MEMORANDUM OF UNDERSTANDING

Collaborations. Some people hate 'em and some people (especially funders!) love 'em. Which group do you belong to? Even if you count yourself among the "collabora-phobics," you'll probably have to accept the fact that various kinds of partnerships are a permanent part of the landscape in the nonprofit world. Among the challenges of these affiliations is making sure all the parties understand and agree on the details of how the arrangement will work. It's essential that all parties in the collaboration be in clear agreement on the specifics before you start submitting funding applications and certainly before the project begins. A good memo of understanding can meet that challenge, and when included as a proposal attachment, it will also reassure potential funders that the venture will run smoothly.

The following checklist uses examples based on the proposal for the Senior Dental Access Project from Chapter Nine, which will help you craft memos of understanding for your own collaborations.

- *Title and purpose of the document.* For example, **Title:** Memorandum of Understanding between the University of Mars School of Dentistry, Sedgwick Elder Care Services, and Blue Moon Senior Care Alliance for the Senior Dental Access Project, a Collaborative Project. **Purpose:** This memorandum is meant to clarify and define the responsibilities of and working relationship between the undersigned agencies regarding distribution of grant funds for the Senior Dental Access Project and the fiscal and programmatic accountability for the use of those funds.

- *Brief description of the mission and programs of each participating agency.* For example, "The University of Mars School of Dentistry (UMSD) was established in 1955 and has graduated some of the top dentists and orthodontists in the state. Currently, UMSD trains 300 students for careers in dentistry and as dental hygienists and an additional 75 postdoctoral students. Sedgwick Elder Care Services (Sedgwick), founded in 1973, is the county's largest provider of adult day care and in-home care, currently serving 1,100 clients. Blue Moon Senior Care Alliance (the Alliance) is affiliated with Galaxy Senior Alliance Centers, a national operator of residential senior communities. The Alliance operates several long-term senior-care facilities in the county, serving 622 residents."

- *Statement of purpose for the collaboration and a description of the project's services, target area, and clients.* For example, "The purpose of the Senior Dental Access Project is to address the dental-health needs of homebound seniors and those living in long-term care facilities in Blue Moon County."

- *Chart of responsibilities showing all project components and which agency is responsible for each.* For example, "The program components and the partner responsible for each is shown in the chart below."

Chart of Responsibilities

University of Mars School of Dentistry	Sedgwick Elder Care Services	Blue Moon Senior Care Alliance
Dental care	Outreach	Space for dental clinics
Assistance in preparing materials for outreach	Patient scheduling	Access to residents at Alliance facilities
Solicitation of in-kind donations of equipment and supplies	Access to home care clients	
Fiscal services		

- *A description of fiscal procedures and accountability.* For example, "All funds for this project are restricted for use in the program described in the accompanying proposal. UMSD will be the fiscal agent for this project and will receive all funds for disbursement. Sedgwick Elder Care Services and the Alliance will submit time sheets and documentation for reimbursement for project expenses to UMSD on a monthly basis."

• *Organizational chart showing staffing and reporting relationships.* For example, "Reporting relationships of all project staff are indicated in the chart below. In addition, to ensure the smooth functioning of the Senior Dental Access Project, a management team consisting of the Outreach Coordinator/Scheduler for the Project; the UMSD Professor of Geriatric Dentistry who will be supervising dental students; and the Health Services Director for the Alliance will be formed and will meet monthly to review progress." See the chart below.

Organizational Chart

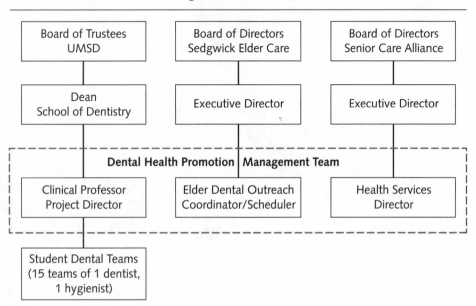

• *Description of reporting requirements.* For example, "UMSD personnel will track clients and dental services provided through the project. UMSD will forward summary reports of the number of patients served and the number and type of services provided to the outreach coordinator or scheduler each month. Sedgwick and the Alliance will each track the number of their clients who are served through the program. They will also provide demographic information on clients to the outreach coordinator or scheduler each month. Outcome data will be provided to the project management team on a quarterly basis."

• *Statement of fiscal and lead agency responsibilities.* For example, "UMSD agrees to (1) reimburse Sedgwick and the Alliance in a timely fashion for all properly submitted project expenses, (2) comply with funding and other contractual agreements, (3) arrange for an annual audit on the use of funds, and (4) provide Sedgwick and the Alliance with a financial statement for the project on a quarterly basis."

• *Statement of subcontracting agency responsibilities.* For example, "Sedgwick and the Alliance agree to comply with all funding and other contractual obligations, and they will provide information needed for reporting requirements in a timely fashion."

• *Signatures of executive officers or board chairs (sometimes both) of each participating agency.*

RESOURCE B: GRANTMAKERS RESPONDING TO OUR SURVEY

Please note that each grantmaker is listed with the foundation or other funder they represented at the time of our survey in the fall of 2005; some have since moved to other positions. We are most grateful to the following colleagues from the nonprofit world who so generously shared their wisdom from "the other side of the desk."

Linda Appleton, The Health Trust, San Jose, California

Marcia Argyris, McKesson Foundation, San Francisco, California

Janice Astbury, The J. W. McConnell Family Foundation, Montreal, Quebec

M. Carlota Baca, New Mexico Association of Grantmakers, Santa Fe, New Mexico

Pam Baker, Woods Charitable Fund, Lincoln, Nebraska

Dave Beckwith, The Needmor Fund, Toledo, Ohio

Sister Janet Burkhart, HM, Sisters of the Humility of Mary, Villa Maria, Pennsylvania

Grace Caliendo, John Muir/Mt. Diablo Community Health Fund, Walnut Creek, California

Martha Campbell, The James Irvine Foundation, San Francisco and Los Angeles, California

Carole Chamberlain, California Endowment, Los Angeles, California

Alice Cottingham, Girl's Best Friend Foundation, Chicago, Illinois

Laurie Craft, Grand Rapids Community Foundation, Grand Rapids, Michigan

Rene O. Deida, Prudential Foundation, Newark, New Jersey

Adeeba Deterville, Citibank Community Relations, San Francisco, California

Mario Diaz, Wells Fargo Foundation, San Francisco, California

Christine Elbel, Fleishhacker Foundation, San Francisco, California

Jan Eldred, California HealthCare Foundation, Oakland, California

Virginia Elliott, United Methodist Health Ministry Fund, Hutchinson, Kansas

Liesel Fenner, New England Foundation for the Arts, Boston, Massachusetts

Diane Ford, Sobrato Foundation, Cupertino, California

Donna Gassie, Virginia Tobacco Settlement Foundation, Richmond, Virginia

Mary Gregory, Pacific Foundation Services, San Francisco, California

Sandra P. Guthman, Polk Bros. Foundation, Chicago, Illinois

Aaron Jacobs, Social Venture Partners, Seattle, Washington

Barbara Jacobs, Plough Foundation, Memphis, Tennessee

Ronald D. Jones, Siebert Lutheran Foundation, Inc., Wauwatosa, Wisconsin

Barbara Kemmis, Crossroads Fund, Chicago, Illinois

Pam LeRose, West Virginia Humanities Council, Charleston, West Virginia

Elizabeth M. Lynch, Massachusetts Bar Foundation, Boston, Massachusetts

Nora Maloy, Blue Cross and Blue Shield of Michigan Foundation, Detroit, Michigan

Jan Masaoka, CompassPoint Nonprofit Services, San Francisco, California

Joan McCammon, The J. W. McConnell Family Foundation, Montreal, Quebec

Lori McGlinchey, Open Society Institute, New York, New York

Ann McQueen, Boston Foundation, Boston, Massachusetts

Ricardo Millett, Woods Fund of Chicago, Illinois

Judith Murphy, Y and H Soda Foundation, Orinda, California

Catherine T. O'Brien, William J. and Dorothy K. O'Neill Foundation Inc., Cleveland, Ohio

Matthew O'Grady, Taproot Foundation, San Francisco, California

Randy Okamura, SBC Foundation, San Francisco, California

Lina Paredes, Liberty Hill Foundation, Los Angeles, California

Frances Phillips, Walter and Elise Haas Fund, San Francisco, California

James R. Posner, Posner-Wallace Foundation, Potomac, Maryland

David Steven Rappoport, Maine Health Access Foundation, Augusta, Maine

Andrea L. Reynolds, Community Foundation of Greater Memphis, Tennessee

Dolores Roybal, Santa Fe Community Foundation, Santa Fe, New Mexico

Lynne Rumball, The Greater Tacoma Community Foundation, Tacoma, Washington

Diane Sanchez, East Bay Community Foundation, Oakland, California

Laura Sanford, SBC Foundation, San Antonio, Texas

Barbara Silzle, Leeway Foundation, Philadelphia, Pennsylvania

Sandra Sinclair, The J. W. McConnell Family Foundation, Montreal, Quebec

Allen Smart, Rapides Foundation, Alexandria, Louisiana

Michell Speight, Dyson Foundation, Millbrook, New York

Molly Talbot-Metz, Mary Black Foundation, Spartanburg, South Carolina

Cheryl Taylor, Foellinger Foundation, Fort Wayne, Indiana

Chet Tchozewski, Global Greengrants Fund, Boulder, Colorado

Karen Topakian, Agape Foundation, San Francisco, California

Sandra Treacy, W. Clement & Jessie V. Stone Foundation, San Francisco, California

Mary Vallier-Kaplan, Endowment for Health, Concord, New Hampshire

Anne Vally, The James Irvine Foundation, San Francisco and Los Angeles, California

Dana Vocisano, The J. W. McConnell Family Foundation, Montreal, Quebec

Robert Walker, Frank H. and Eva B. Buck Foundation, Vacaville, California

Carole M. Watson, United Way of the Bay Area, San Francisco, California

Molly White, Nike, Beaverton, Oregon

Nancy Wiltsek, Pottruck Family Foundation, San Francisco, California

Judith L. Woodruff, Northwest Health Foundation, Portland, Oregon

Carolyn Young, Hogg Foundation for Mental Health, Austin, Texas

Jacqueline Young, Langendorf Foundation, San Francisco, California

Denise San Antonio Zeman, Saint Luke's Foundation of Cleveland, Ohio

Kathy Zundel, Sisters of Mercy of the Americas, St. Louis Regional Community, St. Louis, Missouri

INDEX

A

Agape Foundation, 35, 189

Agencies: "fitting" grantmakers and, 5–19; 501(c)(3) letter of, 22, 189–190, 193; including statistics from your, 77; size, history, and sophistication of, 98. *See also* Applicants

American Dental Association, 140

American Diabetes Association, 70

Anderson Family Foundation: guidelines of, 7–9; letter of inquiry to, 10–19

Appleton, L., 59, 84

Applicants: fitting mission of grantmaker and, 6; importance of following the guidelines, 5–9; letter of inquiry by, 10–19. *See also* Agencies; Proposals

Argus County Community Fund, 64

Argus County homelessness, 54–57, 64–67

Arts organizations: challenges of evaluating, 98–99; Needs Statement dilemma of, 62–63

Ashbury, J., 186

Attachments: board of directors list, 190–191; decisions on whether or not to include, 191–192; 501(c)(3) letter, 22, 189–190, 193

Authoring issues: florid writing, 151–166; "Frankenstein" proposals by multiple authors, 127–128; grantwriting tips on, 137; importance of consistency, 148–149; making sense of nonsense, 167–184; redundancy and inconsistency, 128–137; Senior Dental Access examples of, 129–135, 139–149; staying organized in collaboration, 137–149; transforming your proposal, 195–197. *See also* Writing styles

Authors. *See* Multiple authors

B

Baca, M. C., 50

Beckwith, D., 53

Betsy Ross Elementary School, 25, 28

Bird, L. M., 67

Blue Moon County, 129–135, 139–149

Board of directors list, 190

Boston Foundation, 61, 91, 93, 106

Boyd, F., 190

Bridges to Nature proposal, 10–11, 15–17

Buck Foundation, 76

Budget section: decision on whether to balance or not the, 110–111; final recommendations on, 111–112;

Budget section, *continued*
grantmaker complaints about, 111; grantmaker expectations regarding, 101; grantwriting tips on, 103, 104, 106, 107; importance of financial details in, 105–106; including the revenue in, 104–105; matching the words with the dollars in, 103–104; narratives included in the, 106–107; Partnership for Progress, 57, 102*t*; providing revised budgets in, 107–110; spotting financial flaws in, 102–103

Burkhart, Sister J., 61, 90, 187, 190

Busloads to Bridges program, 16–17, 18

C

Caliendo, G., 53, 184, 186

California HealthCare Foundation, 91, 105

CALM (Community Art and Literacy Museum) proposal: initial version of, 153–161; revamped, 162–166

Census demographic data, 68

Charles W. La Due Family Fund, 129, 139

Charts, 187–188

Citibank, 187

Citibank Community Relations, 60

Clarke, C. A., 101

Client stories: great debate over using, 59; pros and cons of using, 59–62

Collaborating authors. *See* Authoring issues

Communication: importance of crystal clear, 183–184; lofty vocabulary/noble phrases impact on, 175–176; writing as you speak, 176

Community Foundation of Greater Memphis, 24, 137

Cottingham, A., 58, 61, 85

County Social Services and Crisis Intervention, 54, 64

Craft, L., 81, 152

Crossroads Fund, 50, 60, 84, 186, 188

D

Demographics: using census data on, 68; Polaris County, 72*t*–73*t*

Deterville, A., 60, 187

Diabetes Education Program proposal: Evaluation section initially used in, 89–91; Evaluation section makeover used in, 94–97; Goals and Objectives section initially used in, 86–88, 89; Goals and Objectives section makeover used in, 94–97; statistics initially used in, 70–77; statistics used in makeover version, 77–82

Diaz, M. P., 13, 76

Display material, 187–189

Dyson Foundation, 60

E

East Bay Community Foundation, 76

Elbel, C., 50, 188

Eldred, J., 91

Ella Hogans Community Resources, Inc., 54, 57, 64

Elliott, V., 60, 76, 91–92, 137

Elred, J., 105

Endowment for Health, 91, 106, 188

Evaluation. *See* Program Evaluation section

F

Fellowship House proposal, 121–125

Fenner, L., 19, 38, 60, 98–99

"The Fit": definition of, 6; four factors of, 6–7; letter of inquiry makeover for, 14–19; using the guidelines to find, 5–6; wrapping up, 19

501(c)(3) letter, 22, 189–190, 193

Fleishhacker Foundation, 50, 188

Florid writing: CALM proposal example of, 153–161; CALM proposal rewritten without, 162–166; grantmakers on annoyance of, 151–152; grantwriting tip on avoiding, 158, 159, 160; recommendations regarding, 166; specific problems caused by, 158–160

Foellinger Foundation, 97, 152

Folse, G., 140

Fonts, 185–186, 187

Ford, D., 50

Foundation guidelines: letter of inquiry following, 10–11; mirroring language of the, 7; sample, 7–9; used to make "the fit," 5–6

Frank H. and Eva B. Buck Foundation, 76

"Frankenstein" proposals, 127–128

Funders. *See* Grantmakers

Future Funding section: HSoHK proposal, 173, 182; Knitting for Nippers, 34–35; tips on length of, 120

G

Gassie, D., 128, 189

Girl's Best Friend Foundation, 58, 61, 85

Goals: funder ambivalence over requesting, 84; objectives versus, 84. *See also* Objectives

Goals and Objectives section: described, 21, 23; Diabetes Education Program proposal, 86–88, 89–91; funder ambivalence over requesting, 84; good planning reflected in, 93; grantwriting tips on, 87, 88; HSoHK proposal, 171, 179; Partnership for Progress Homeless Program proposal, 55; as setting program standards, 85; summing up on the, 99. *See also* Objectives

Grand Rapids Community Foundation, 81, 152

Grant size, 98

Grantmakers: budget section expectations/complaints by, 101, 111; on client stories and testimonials use, 59–62; fitting your agency and, 6–19; on florid writing as annoying, 151–152; importance of Needs Statement to, 52–53; "know your funder" rules on, 196–197; making an impression on the, 5–19; meeting the polled, 2–3; obtaining copy of most current guidelines of, 5–6; process versus outcome evaluation preferences by, 97–98; on statistics as Needs Statement element, 69; unique nature of different, 196

Grantwriting tips: on accessing demographic census data, 68; on anticipating questions and providing answers, 175; on avoiding florid writing, 158, 159, 160; on budget narratives, 107; checking and proofing your work, 14; on financial details to include, 105; importance of impression made by proposals, 39; on inconsistencies, 137; on matching proposal information and budget, 104; on Objectives and Goals section, 87, 88; on proposal length, 120; show that your agency fits, 13; on showing revenue in the budget, 104; on typefaces and fonts, 187; on using calculators to check the math, 103; on using statistics, 76; what to include in a Needs Statement, 62; on writing as you speak, 176

Graphs, 187–188

The Greater Tacoma Community Foundation, 50

Gregory, M., 12, 53, 91, 93, 105, 187, 192

Gregory Norwood Family Foundation (Knitting for Nippers): initial proposal of, 25–40; remixing the proposal, 40–50

Guidelines. *See* Foundation guidelines

H

Haas Fund, 18, 61

The Health Trust, 59, 84

History and Mission section: described, 23; Knitting for Nippers initial, 25–28; Knitting for Nippers makeover, 41–42; tips on length of, 120

Hogg Foundation for Mental Health, 23, 188

Homeless Resource Center proposal (Partnership for Progress): Needs Statement of, 54–58, 64–67; proposed revised budget in, 108*t*–109*t*

HSoHK (High School of Hard Knocks) proposal: initial version of, 169–176; makeover version of, 176–184

I

Impacts, 92

Inconsistency issue, 128–137

Information overload, 75–76

Inputs, 92

IRS 501(c)(3) letter, 22, 189–190, 193

J

Jacobs, A., 12, 52–53, 59, 98, 168, 190

Jacobs, B., 50, 59

The James Irvine Foundation, 60, 105, 185, 188

John Muir/Mt. Diablo Community Health Fund, 53, 184, 186

J.W. McConnell Family Foundation, 12, 52, 58, 75, 159, 186

K

Kemmis, B., 50, 60, 84, 186, 188

Knitting for Nippers: initial proposal of, 25–40; remixing the proposal, 40–50

"Know your funder" rules, 196–197

L

Langendorf Foundation, 60, 90

Language issues: lofty vocabulary/noble phrases, 175–176; writing style as, 167–168; writing as you speak, 176

Leeway Foundation, 24, 188

LeRose, P., 24, 99

Letter of inquiry: initial "ugly duckling," 10–11; lack of "fitness" in initial, 12–13; lack of relevant and substantive details, 14; lack of "zing," 14; makeover of initial, 14–19; poor first and lasting misimpression of, 13–14

Liberty Hill Foundation, 76

Logic models, 92

Lydia E. Girande Memorial Clinic proposal: Evaluation section of, 89–91, 94–97; Goals and Objections sections of, 86–88, 94–97; makeover version of, 94–97; use of statistics in, 70–75, 78–82

Lynch, E. M., 38–39, 53, 59, 77, 81, 98, 106, 149, 185

M

McCammon, J., 159

McGlinchey, L., 6, 69, 84, 106, 168

McQueen, A., 61, 91, 93, 106

Maine Health Access Foundation, 24, 60, 62–63, 97

Martia G. Santos Family Foundation, 70

Mary Black Foundation, 106

Massachusetts Bar Foundation, 38, 59, 77, 81, 98, 106, 149, 185

Measurable Outcomes section: described, 50; HSoHK proposal, 173, 181–182; Knitting for Nippers initial, 33–34; Knitting for Nippers makeover, 44–45. *See also* Outcomes

Methods section: HSoHK proposal, 171–172, 179–181; Partnership for Progress, 55–56; tips on length of, 120

Millett, R., 13

Mission statements: fitting grantmaker and your agency's, 6; nonsense writing style of, 167–168; proposal's statement on, 21, 23

Multiple authors. *See* Authoring issues

Murphy, J., 38, 104

"Mystery" proposal: crystal clear communication to avoid, 183–184; grantwriting tips on, 175, 176; HSoHK example of nonsense, 169–176; HSoHK example of revamped, 176–183; writing style of, 167–168

N

The Needmor Fund, 53

Needs: establishing the, 57–58, 62–63; opportunity versus, 63

Needs Statement section: using client stories and testimonials in, 59–62; described, 21, 22, 23, 50; dilemma for arts organizations, 62–63; establishing the need using the, 57–58, 62–63; grantwriting tips on the, 62, 68; as "heart of the proposal," 51, 69; HSoHK proposal, 169–171, 177–179; importance for grantmakers, 52–53; Knitting for Nippers, 21, 22, 23, 29–31, 42–44, 50; "making the case" in the, 51, 68; Partnership for Progress, 54, 57–58, 63, 64–68; statistics as necessary element of, 69, 82; tips on length of, 120. *See also* Proposal sections

New England Foundation for the Arts, 19, 38, 60, 98

New Mexico Association of Grantmakers, 50

Nike, 98, 151

NikeGO grant programs, 98

Noel Norton Foundation, 153

Nonsense. *See* "Mystery" proposal

Northwest Health Foundation, 38, 53, 60, 97, 128

O

Objectives: funder ambivalence regarding, 84; goals versus, 84; process and product, 90, 92; SMART approach to, 87. *See also* Goals; Goals and Objectives section

O'Brien, C. T., 57

Okamura, R., 61, 190

Open Society Institute, 6, 69, 106, 168

Oral Health in America: A Report of the Surgeon General, 140

Outcome evaluation approach, 97–98

Outcomes, 92. *See also* Measurable Outcomes section

Outputs, 92

P

Pacific Foundation Services, 12, 53, 91, 93, 105, 187, 192

Paredes, L., 76

Partnership for Progress proposal: Budget section of, 57, 102*t*, 108*fig*–109*fig*; Needs Statement section of, 54, 57–58, 64–67

Phillips, F., 19, 61

Photographs, 187–189

Pleasantville Interfaith Alliance, 54, 55, 56, 64

Plough Foundation, 50, 59

Polaris County demographics, 72*t*–73*t*

Posner, J. R., 61, 77, 185

Posner-Wallace Foundation, 61, 77, 185

Pottruck Family Foundation, 13, 61, 105

Problem Statement section. *See* Needs Statement section

Process, 92

Process evaluation approach, 97–98

Process objectives, 90, 92

Product objectives, 90, 92

Program Description section: Knitting for Nippers initial, 31–32; Knitting for Nippers makeover, 45–47; Partnership for Progress, 56

Program Evaluation section: Diabetes Education Program proposal, 89–91; good planning reflected in, 93; HSoHK proposal, 173, 181–182; Knitting for Nippers, 32–33, 47; logic models used in, 92; moving beyond bean counting, 91–92; as part of best practices, 85; process versus outcome evaluation approach in, 97–98; summing up for the, 99; tips on length of, 120

Proposal examples: Bridges to Nature, 10–11, 15–17; CALM (Community Art and Literacy Museum), 153–161, 162–166; Fellowship House, 115–125; HSoHK (High School of Hard Knocks), 169–184; Knitting for Nippers, 25–49; Lydia E. Girarde Memorial Clinic Diabetes Program, 70–75, 78–82, 86–91, 94–97; Partnership for Progress Homelessness Program, 54–57, 64–68, 102t; Senior Dental Access, 129–135, 139–149

Proposal (Knitting for Nippers): fixing disorganized, 40–50; History and Mission section of, 23, 25–28, 41–42; jumbled order of "ugly duckling," 35–37; last-minute cut-and-paste job

of initial, 38–40; Measurable Outcomes section of, 33–34, 44–45; Needs (or Problem) Statement of, 21, 22, 23, 29–31, 42–44, 50; positive comments for the initial, 40; Program Description section of, 31–32, 45–47, 31–32, 45–47; Program Evaluation section of, 32–33, 47; reviewing what went wrong with, 37–38; sample of initial, 25–35; second rewritten, 41–48; solid structure of makeover, 49; writing billboard headings in second, 49–50

Proposal length: appropriate details to include in, 120–121; Fellowship House example of just right, 121–125; Fellowship House example of too long, 115–121; final recommendations on, 126; florid writing adding to, 159–160; grantwriting tips on, 120; problems with verbose proposals, 113–114; too much detail adding to, 119–120; too spare and short, 121

Proposal package: attachments to include with, 22, 189–192; charts, graphs, and photographs, 187–189; checklist for, 192–193; final points on preparing, 192; grantwriting tips on preparing the, 187, 189; printing/typeface issues, 185–186; summary of key rules on, 196–197

Proposal sections: Budget, 57, 101–112; Future Funding, 34–35, 120, 173, 182; Goals and Objectives, 21, 23, 55, 83–99, 171; History and Mission, 23, 25–28; Measurable Outcomes, 33–34, 44–45, 50, 173, 181–182; Methods, 55–56, 120, 171–172, 179–181; Program Description, 31–32, 45–47, 56; Program Evaluation, 32–33, 47, 83–99, 120, 173, 181–182; standard sequence

of, 21–22; Summary, 21, 22, 83, 120.
See also Needs Statement section
Proposals: using client stories and testimonials in, 59–62; components in the form of a question, 23; disorganized disasters, 50; evaluating, 83–99; florid writing of, 151–166; "Frankenstein," 127–128; length of, 113–126, 159–160; making sense of nonsense, 167–184; the perfect package, 185–197; poor impression of disorganized, 23–24; RFP (Request for Proposals), 12; using statistics in, 69–82; transforming your, 195–197; written by multiple authors, 127–149. *See also* Applicants

R

Rapides Foundation, 24
Rappoport, D. S., 24, 60, 61, 97
Readability, 186
Reality Grantmaking workshops, 1
Reynolds, A. L., 24, 104, 137
RFP (Request for Proposals), 12
Robert Bisinger Charitable Fund, 115, 122
Roberta Gonzalez Foundation, 54
Roybal, D. E., 38
Rumball, L., 50

S

Saint Luke's Foundation (Cleveland), 24, 61
Sanchez, D., 76
Sanford, L., 106
Santa Fe Community Foundation, 38
SBC Foundation, 106, 190
Senior Dental Access proposal: inconsistencies in, 129–135; organization of rewritten, 139–149
Silzle, B., 24, 188
Sinclair, S., 12, 52, 58, 75
Sisters of the Humility of Mary, 61, 90, 187, 190

Sisters of Mercy of the Americas, St. Louis Regional Community, 186
Smart, A., 24
SMART proposal writing, 87
Sobrato Foundation, 50
Social Venture Partners Seattle, 12, 52, 59, 98, 168, 190
Speight, M., 60
Spell-checking, 13
Statistics: Diabetes Education Program proposal uses of, 70–75, 78–82; grantwriting tip on how to use, 76; including agency, 77; information overload by overusing, 75–76; mastering the use of, 81–82; as necessary Needs Statement element, 69, 82
Stone Foundation, 61, 81, 85, 104
Summary section: described, 21, 22, 83; tips on length of, 120

T

Tactile Textiles: A Sensory Experience exhibit proposal: initial version of, 153–161; revamped version of, 162–166
Talbot-Metz, M., 106
Target population: defining the, 58; demographics of the, 68, 72*t*–73*t*
Taylor, C., 97, 152
Testimonials: great debate over using, 59; pros and cons of using, 59–62
Topakian, K., 35, 189
Treacy, S., 61, 81, 85, 104
Typefaces, 185–186, 187

U

United Methodist Health Ministry Fund, 60, 76, 91, 137
United Way of the Bay Area, 59, 91
Urban Institute, 54

V

Vallier-Kaplan, M., 91, 106, 188
Vally, A., 60, 105, 185, 188
Virginia Tobacco Settlement Foundation, 128, 189
Vocabulary issues, 175–176

W

W. Clement & Jessie V. Stone Foundation, 61, 81, 85, 104
Walker, R., 76
Walter and Elise Haas Fund, 19, 61
Watson, C. M., 59, 91
Website demographic sources, 68
Wells Fargo Foundation, 13, 76
West Polaris County, 70, 72t–75, 86
West Virginia Humanities Council, 24, 99
White, M., 98, 151

William J. & Dorothy K. O'Neill Foundation, 57
Wiltsek, N., 13, 61, 105–106
Woodruff, J. L., 38, 53, 60, 97–98, 128
Woods Fund (Chicago), 13
Writing styles: florid, 151–166; making sense of nonsense, 167–184; problems with academic, 167; writing as you speak, 176. *See also* Authoring issues

Y

Y&H Soda Foundation, 38, 104
Young, C., 23, 188
Young, J., 60, 90

Z

Zeman, D.S.A., 24, 61, 98
Zundel, K., 186